USING COMMUNITY TRANSITION TEAMS TO IMPROVE TRANSITION SERVICES

PRO-ED Series on Transition

Edited by
J. Patton
G. Blalock
C. Dowdy
T. E. C. Smith

USING COMMUNITY TRANSITION TEAMS TO IMPROVE TRANSITION SERVICES

Ginger Blalock
and
Michael R. Benz

8700 Shoal Creek Boulevard
Austin, Texas 78757-6897
800/897-3202 Fax 800/397-7633
Order online at http://www.proedinc.com

8700 Shoal Creek Boulevard
Austin, Texas 78757-6897
800/897-3202 Fax 800/397-7633
Order online at http://www.proedinc.com

Library of Congress Cataloging-in-Publication Data

Blalock, Ginger.
Using community transition teams to improve transition services / Ginger Blalock, Michael R. Benz.
p. cm. — (PRO-ED series on transition)
Includes bibliographical references (p.).
ISBN 0-89079-811-7 (alk. paper)
1. Vocational guidance for the handicapped—United States—Handbooks, manuals, etc. 2. Handicapped young adults—Services for—United States—Handbooks, manuals, etc. 3. School-to-work transition—United States—Handbooks, manuals, etc. 4. Social service—United States—Team work—Handbooks, manuals, etc. I. Benz, Michael R. II. Title. III. Series.
HV1568.5.B55 1999
362.4'048—dc21 98-33327

This book is designed in New Century Schoolbook and Melior.

Printed in the United States of America

4 5 6 7 8 9 10 07 06 05

Contents

Preface to Series

The transition of students from school to adulthood roles has emerged as one of the most important topics in the field of special education and rehabilitation. The critical nature of planning for the transition needs of students has also been recognized in the school-to-work, often referred to as school-to-careers, initiative.

The PRO-ED Series on Transition evolved from a symposium convened in September 1994. Along with the opportunity for professionals interested in the practical aspects of the transition process to discuss many different issues, the symposium produced a series of papers that were published originally in the *Journal of Learning Disabilities* and subsequently in bound form as a book titled *Transition and Students with Learning Disabilities*. The current series represents an attempt to provide practical resources to transition personnel on a variety of topics that are critical to the process of preparing individuals for adulthood. Each book in the series contains valuable practical information on a specific transition topic. Titles in the series include:

- *Adult Agencies: Linkages for Adolescents in Transition*
- *Assessment for Transitions Planning*
- *Developing Transitions Plans*
- *Family Involvement in Transition Planning and Implementation*
- *Follow-Up Studies: A Practitioner's Handbook*
- *Infusing Real-Life Topics into Existing Curricula: Recommended Procedures and Instructional Examples for the Elementary, Middle, and High School Levels*
- *Self-Determination Strategies*
- *Teaching Occupational Social Skills*
- *Transition from School to Young Adulthood: Basic Concepts and Recommended Practices*
- *Transition Issues Related to Students with Visual Disabilities*
- *Transition to Employment*
- *Using Community Transition Teams To Improve Transition Services*
- *Working with Students with Disabilities in Vocational–Technical Settings*

We hope that these resources will add to the growing body of materials designed to assist professionals involved in the transition process. The books in this series address the need for practical resources on transition that focus solely on specific topics.

Jim Patton, Ginger Blalock, Carol Dowdy, Tom Smith

CHAPTER 1
The Roles of Community Transition Teams

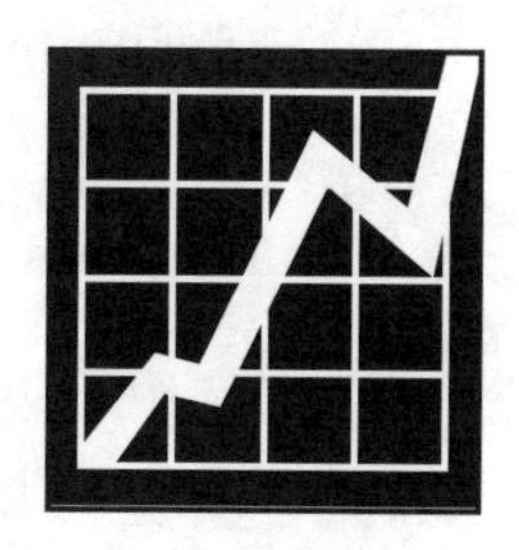

INTRODUCTION

Students, families, human service professionals, and community members across the United States—and probably you—share a common goal: All students will leave school systems equipped to be successful, interdependent adults. Many of these same stakeholders also share an emerging understanding that schools cannot achieve this goal alone. As a result, students' transitions from K–12 education systems to the challenges of adulthood have become a major focus in our society, and a great deal has been learned from examining this process. One discovery is that transition planning and services are especially important for students with special needs, including disabilities. Also, many partners, coming from very different arenas, are needed to create the school-based and community-based experiences that students need in order to *prepare* for all of life's domains. These domains include employment, education, home and family living, physical and mental health, community participation, recreation and leisure, and personal responsibility and relationships (Cronin & Patton, 1993). Numerous partners also are needed to create the employment and adult support options to which students move after high school. Many communities and states have learned that the local or community transition team (CTT) is a helpful, even essential, vehicle for bringing together key stakeholders to develop needed transition services and programs. Frankly, we believe that *all* the transition services and program components featured in the Transition Series—such as individualized transition plans, work-related social skills instruction, transition assessment, and follow-along studies—are more readily facilitated through community transition teams.

Community transition teams, because of their missions and their members, are capable of producing important results, particularly in the area of creating solutions to the barriers that students face. For example, community transition teams may work to generate transportation options, to connect educators with employers for training options, or to lobby legislators for increased adult services. A great deal more can be accomplished by several thinkers who represent diverse perspectives and realms of authority than by a few with similar backgrounds.

Emerging community transition teams face some formidable tasks, as do all important groups. Potential team members have to find each other, identify a compelling reason to work together, figure out how to work together, and sustain the collaboration long enough to achieve an agreed upon outcome. Enough communities and states have worked through this process so that we now know what steps to take. This manual was created to share what has been learned. Its contents spell out the stages and activities that have proven important in creating and maintaining a collaborative group focused on school-to-careers transitions. The purpose of this manual is to teach you—whether you are starting with 2 people or 20 people who share your commitment—how to form and support a local team that will facilitate improved transition programs and lead to better student outcomes than schools alone can generate.

This manual portrays the stages of team development and long-term effectiveness through the remaining six chapters:

- Chapter 2 Building a Team That Represents the Community
- Chapter 3 Setting the Team Up for Success
- Chapter 4 Identifying the Community's Highest Priority Needs
- Chapter 5 Developing an Effective Plan of Action
- Chapter 6 Implementing the Action Plan
- Chapter 7 Evaluating and Building on Accomplishments

This manual describes the strategies and experiences of a range of communities across the United States who have built community transition teams, including numerous towns, counties, and regions. No matter what size the community, those groups found their transition teams to be instrumental in creating critical opportunities for students' educational experiences and linkages to adult systems. The education profession and its partners are still learning what works, and what (sometimes) does not work, in supporting smooth transitions. Therefore, we invite you to share with us additional strategies that may not be presented here, as we all strive to improve students' outcomes.

BENEFITS

Community transition teams, regardless of their geographic, economic, or cultural landscapes, offer numerous advantages to students and key stakeholders. The numbers, composition, mission, and activities of each team work together to help agencies and individuals progress toward stated goals. Some of the reasons you should consider developing a community transition team are listed here.

- The true nature of a community's goals regarding transition and related services emerge when the team is representative of the community. Given sufficient time and a supportive climate, the opportunity is created for key voices to be heard and for all critical factors to be considered. The community transition team can be the means of constructing a uniquely designed service delivery system to meet local needs.
- The team serves as a vehicle for identifying and clarifying the roles and opportunities of other stakeholder groups and their members. Each group can share its role responsibilities, the constraints under which it operates, and the "doors" that it can help open or advance.
- A representative group working together is more likely to use what is already in place (existing systems, structures, and services) and to maximize everyone's involvement, if resources are scarce as is typical in rural communities (Helge, 1991).
- The team's membership boosts the credibility of emerging school-to-careers activities. School personnel alone will have a hard time convincing the community that they are on the most strategic path for the community's economic well-being.
- The team's activities allow all participants to "own" the process and program. Each member can articulate ideas and concerns and can help shape the plan that emerges.

- Sharing responsibilities and ownership among many members means that accountability and follow-through are heightened, leading to better options and outcomes for students.
- The team's composition affords reality checks for participants who are trying to understand the big picture. Members can dispel myths or misconceptions and offer firsthand information.
- Many minds, meeting for many hours over time, will inherently generate more and better ideas than would just a few people or a group whose members are all "shaped from the same mold." Supported brainstorming will eventually help a group think "outside of the box." One radio interviewee recently recommended 2 to 3 hours of unfettered brainstorming by 20 or more people in order to produce truly creative ideas. Participants tend to build on each statement and ultimately generate suggestions that would never have emerged without the contributions of the entire group.
- The team process provides a structure that helps members feel comfortable about belonging and taking risks. Over time, members develop a sense of trust that allows them to share more.
- The team's efforts "encourage employers to become school-to-careers advocates through their involvement in the development of the local partnership" (Mahler & Brustein, 1997, pp. 2–4).
- The team may be the primary (or perhaps even only) vehicle for helping the two major career development movements—transition systems change projects and school-to-work initiatives—work together to bring needed change. A recent National Transition Network (NTN) survey found that the *primary collaborative activity* linking personnel from both programs, when they existed in the same state, was *membership on an interagency committee or advisory board* (National Transition Network, 1996–1997).
- A large team membership means that the group's work can be distributed across many people instead of a few. Most community transition teams find that forming subcommittees and/or task forces to focus on specific areas or tasks works well for pushing progress forward.

TEAM FUNCTIONS

This section provides basic information about the purpose, major roles, and typical activities of community transition teams.

Purpose

The ultimate aim of community transition teams (CTTs) is to enhance, develop, and support effective transition programs and services for students. The intermediate purpose is "to provide structured support for local control" (Benz, Lindstrom, Halpern, & Rothstrom, 1991, p. 2). While education serves as the lead agency in transition due to its mandate to educate students for future educational and employment demands, educators have neither the time nor the capacity to achieve those outcomes single-handedly. By generating ideas, tackling barriers, and opening doors, the local team can provide the mechanism through which such student outcomes are achievable. The idea of inviting community partners to scrutinize a school's instructional program and to share in decision making can be unsettling to some educators who are unaccustomed to operating in this manner. The team, however, can become a safe avenue through which those activities can occur because the members develop a sense of mutual understanding and trust as they identify shared goals and meet regularly over a long period of time.

Roles

Table 1.1 outlines several major functions of CTTs. In this manual, some of these functions are presented as key stages of developing and enhancing local teams, while others are actually tasks or targeted outcomes of the group. These functions represent the major work for which a community transition team should be responsible. Each team can identify and shape its major functions, based upon local strengths and needs.

Activities

Exemplary transition programs include a number of key components that best occur through a local team's efforts. Following is a list of the key components of transition programs and the sample activities that community transition teams use to develop those components (Transition Assistance Project, 1997b, 1998a, 1998b).

Key Transition Components	Example Activities of CTTs
Planning within the local context; taking into account community customs, strengths, and gaps	Establish a district strategic planning process, with required community participation (see New Mexico's mandated process in Appendix A).
Active involvement of students and school leavers with disabilities	Create a Student Connection group; conduct follow-up and follow-along studies; host a Futures Conference at an area college where high school students can discuss transition issues and learn about options.
Active involvement of family members	Establish a Parents as Partners program or a Families as Faculty program; encourage parent participation in students' Futures Conference.
School and employer partnerships	Host career talks and career fairs; set up workplace tours, job shadowing or rotations, and internships; provide opportunities for cooperative education, apprenticeships, mentoring, and business practice advisement; encourage curricular input; offer project-based learning and educator externships.
Identification and sharing of school and community resources	Establish a traveling education and awareness package; develop formal interagency agreements (see example in Appendix B); set up a legislative task force on specific issues; publish a local directory in multiple languages; host a career day for youth that also teaches about community education programs (recreation and leisure, home living) and area services; jointly create and fund a home for teaching independent living skills to 18- to 21-year-olds.

Collaboration across the general, vocational, bilingual/multicultural, and special education fields	Establish a building- or district-level curriculum planning and revision committee; set up Individualized Education Program (IEP) committees.

TABLE 1.1

The Major Functions of Community Transition Teams

- Team Development
- Community Needs Assessment
- Action Plans
- Education, Training, and Employment Opportunities
- Professional Development and Technical Assistance
- Interagency Collaboration and Shared Resources
- Monitoring and Evaluating Team Progress

CHAPTER 2
Building a Team That Represents the Community

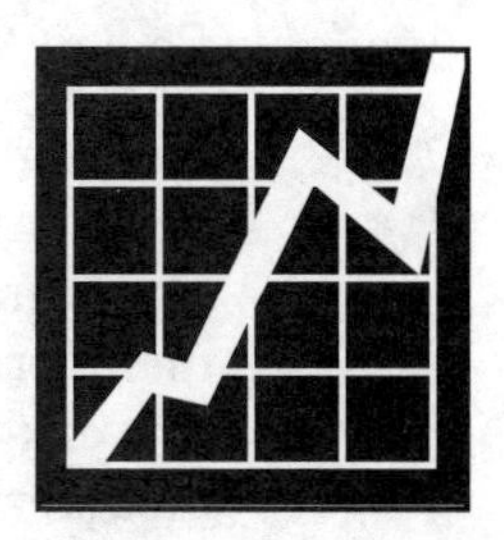

The primary purpose of team building is to establish a strong, cohesive team that represents the community. Once teams are established, team building becomes an ongoing process—teams add new members as they identify new or different priorities for improving services within their community, as members move in and out of the area, or as turnover in positions occurs. The size and location of the community will be a primary consideration in determining the team's framework and composition. Each transition team is unique. A team's geographical boundaries may range from one county with a single school district to several counties with many school districts, or any combination thereof, depending on a number of factors that are described in this chapter.

The team building process involves three major components: (a) developing a team that represents the community; (b) orienting the new team members to the community transition team process, and (c) maintaining the team over time. The first two components are addressed during the early stages of the team building process. The third component, team maintenance, occurs on an ongoing basis throughout the life of the team.

TEAM DEVELOPMENT

The initial development of a community transition team usually involves two activities: (a) establishing an appropriate geopolitical framework for the team, and (b) identifying people who are willing and able to serve as team members.

Establish the Framework

The manner in which you define the basic geographical and organizational boundaries of the transition team will tremendously impact the team's ultimate success in the community. Therefore, undertake this step with careful consideration. Each team will develop a unique framework for establishing team boundaries that meets the needs of its local community. An example might be that some rural areas form *both local* (town or district) *and regional* (possibly county) transition teams, so that all local areas can benefit from the successes and resources of the other areas. Team membership may also vary greatly according to the needs of the community. The size and location of the community affects in several ways how the team may be structured. Factors include: (a) the available pool of participants; (b) competition for resources; (c) logistics imposed by the distance between agencies, families, and organizations that you wish to include; and (d) the number of school districts with secondary special education programs.

Available Pool of Participants

The number of teachers, service providers, family members, employers, and others who may be available to serve on the team will vary according to the size of the community. Larger communities will obviously have a greater pool of potential members than smaller ones. Smaller communities tend to enlist the same persons to work on a multitude of committees, which runs the risk of overextended team members. However, that sometimes can be an advantage; if the mission of an existing team or committee closely relates to an emerging mission, the extant team may be interested in adding or shifting to the new focus. One example of this might be an economic development task force that is zeroing in on employment opportunities for youth. Another might be a community or regional group who is shifting segregated work placements to integrated or supported employment, and who subsequently recognizes the need for a broader, transition focus.

Several other facets of availability warrant careful consideration if the aim is to create a team that represents the entire community. These facets include:

- socioeconomic differences
- availability of transportation to attend meetings
- language differences
- ethnic and cultural differences
- support needs of potential members with disabilities

Regardless of community size, team members must *want* to participate, since the work being done is entirely voluntary. Community transition teams are typically inviting; they are effective at incorporating diverse issues, materials, and communication styles (Transition Assistance Project, 1996a).

Competition for Resources

The size and location of the community often determines the degree of competition for resources, and this must be taken into account in the development of the transition team. The following example illustrates this point. Imagine that the team is located in an urban area and has chosen to include only one of the three local school districts on the team. The team has decided to work on identifying competitive employment placements for students with disabilities. However, the other two districts are calling on the same employers, and the team finds itself in direct competition with them. Therefore, the team should be structured in such a manner that its interactions with employers do not compete with the interactions of people from the other two school districts. As an alternative strategy, the team could attempt to include members from all three school districts so that the possibility of unwanted competition can be avoided more easily. Similar situations frequently arise in areas where secondary programs and adult agencies seek training and employment sites among the same group of employers.

Logistics Imposed by Distance

The distance between the school districts, agencies, families, and employers represented on the team will have an impact on the logistics of operating the team. For example, teams located in rural communities with great distances between school districts, adult agencies, and community members may find it difficult to meet on a regular basis. Such logistics must be considered when developing a meeting structure and work plan.

Number of Districts with Secondary Special Education Programs

The team will need to decide whether to involve a single school district or multiple school districts. In deciding the number of school districts to include, think about the needs of each school district. Would working together as a team expedite the process of building a quality program in the area, or are the needs of the various districts so different that working separately would prove more efficient? One possibility is to begin with a single school district and expand the team to include additional districts after the team is well established.

As decisions are made about the team's basic framework, remember that the goal is to establish a framework for representation that is sensitive to the geographical and political opportunities and realities present within the community. These decisions are not irrevocable, but they do provide a foundation for identifying those people who will serve as the team's first members.

Identify Team Members

When deciding who to include on the team, strive for a balance between school personnel and non-school personnel to ensure adequate representation on the team. At a minimum, the team should include representatives from the following major categories: (a) school personnel, (b) consumers, (c) adult services personnel, and (d) community members. The list of potential participants included in Table 2.1 will help you determine the representative positions that you would like to include on the team.

There are basically three ways to identify the potential people to serve on the community transition team. The first is to brainstorm with other interested persons or already identified team members who were recruited based on your personal contacts. The second is to contact the agencies that you want represented and ask each agency to select a representative to serve on the team. If you choose this second method, be sure that the persons selected to represent the agency are motivated to become involved. Otherwise, they may quickly lose interest or have little energy to contribute. A third strategy is to convene an initial core group of stakeholders to identify critical needs and then ask them to nominate members who can help accomplish the mission of the team.

Recruitment Strategies

A few recruitment strategies might prove useful to the team. Here are several suggestions to consider:

- Invite anyone who comes to mind, especially the "movers and shakers" in the area.
- Have the first (and perhaps all) meeting(s) at a well-known place; for instance, luncheon meetings at a local restaurant are often successful.
- Always provide refreshments, and advertise that fact.
- Advertise the supports that will be provided (e.g., child care, translators, interpreters).
- Try to arrange for college credit for participating high school students, college students, or teachers on emergency licensure waivers, or for continuing education units (CEUs) for others who might need it.

TABLE 2.1
Suggested Transition Team Members

School Personnel

- Special education teachers
- Regular education teachers
- Vocational education teachers
- School administrators
- Special education administrators
- Transition specialists or coordinators
- Other school personnel (e.g., counselors, related services personnel)
- School board members

Consumers

- Students or school leavers with a disability
- Parents and other family members

Adult Services Personnel

- Vocational rehabilitation counselors
- Mental health case managers
- Vocational and Residential service providers
- Private Industry Council representatives
- Department of Labor representatives
- Postsecondary education and training representatives (including Special Services)
- Corrections personnel
- Other adult agency representatives (e.g., social services)

Community Members

- Employers
- Chamber of Commerce
- Ministerial Association
- Recreation and leisure program personnel
- Local government representatives, including tribal governments
- Other community representatives (e.g., Rotary Club, newspaper, trade organizations)

- Ask agencies to support their staff's involvement and possibly build it into job descriptions.
- Try to arrange for the school to offer a service to the community in some related manner; for example, Accounting II students could set up bookkeeping systems for local small businesses as part of their work-based learning experience.
- Hold preliminary meetings in targeted sites to explain the purpose of the broader team meetings while in an environment that is familiar to the audience (e.g., tribal chapter houses, churches, or the area chamber of commerce). Ask a liaison within a target group (such as the parent of a youth with disabilities or the education director for a pueblo) to initially contact potential members to explain the purpose of the upcoming meeting and efforts.

Don't be afraid to have too many people attend the team meetings, especially in the beginning. You want to maximize input, and allowing lots of people to participate at the start strengthens the community's ownership of the process and its commitment to the outcomes. Also, what tends to happen is that, even if there are 50 or more at the first meeting, the number of those who attend regular meetings and who work on subcommittee tasks is much smaller.

TEAM ORIENTATION

Once potential team members have been identified, they must be contacted in order to determine their willingness to participate. For those who express interest, the process of team building begins to unfold through a team orientation meeting. Several guidelines are suggested here for how to contact potential members and how to conduct the team orientation meeting.

Begin by contacting each potential team member by telephone. Briefly describe possible reasons for their participation. These explanations can focus on a number of possible points, including the following:

- Special education and transition programs in the community are good, but when students leave high school, they are still not prepared to function adequately in the adult world. They face many problems, such as unemployment or underemployment, loneliness, and a lack of independent living skills.
- A community transition team can address these problems effectively because team members will work to develop program improvements that will result in solutions for individual students. Team members will represent the different persons and agencies that have a stake in the outcomes being pursued.
- The emphasis will be on a transition team for this community, developing programs and solutions that work *here*. The team will not be asked to adopt someone else's plan, which may or may not reflect how things work in this community.

Choose any of these explanations that you think may be helpful, or invent others of your own. End the conversation by asking if the person is willing to attend the first meeting of the community transition team to learn more about it. Also ask each person to indicate the most convenient times to attend such a meeting.

After the potential membership has been polled, you will be able to select the best time for the orientation meeting. Send each potential team member a written notice of the meeting place, time, and agenda. The day before the meeting, follow up the written notice with a telephone call to each person to determine if he or she is still planning to attend. If not, ascertain whether the person has a time conflict or is simply no longer interested in participating. The meeting itself will be primarily an explanation of the transition team process and will provide potential team members with an opportunity to reevaluate their commitment to participating.

TEAM MAINTENANCE

Once the team is established, the issue will constantly arise about how to maintain appropriate leadership and membership in order to keep the team active, productive, and happy. This is no easy task! The life of any organization has its ups and downs, and this is especially true for a group of volunteers. The team will need to develop procedures for selecting (or reaffirming) its leader, and for identifying and orienting new members who may join the team.

Appoint a Team Leader

The team leader is the heart of the community transition team process. When the team leader is active, enthusiastic, and organized, the team typically responds with successful efforts and impact. Each team must develop its own procedures for selecting its leadership, and no single pattern for doing this has yet emerged. Our only advice would be that each team should decide upon its own procedures for selecting a leader within its first year of operation.

Regardless of the procedures that are adopted, there are certain characteristics that are needed in the person who serves as team leader. A team leader should be someone who has leadership ability and who also is in a leadership role in the community that relates in some respect to secondary special education and school-to-careers transition programs. The person should be aware of the time commitment necessary for carrying out the role of team leader. Although the amount of time will vary greatly depending on the phase of the model being implemented, the size of the transition team, and the amount of assistance available (such as clerical support), team leaders spend an average of 4 to 8 hours per month performing their transition team duties. Perhaps most important, the team leader should be enthusiastic about assuming this responsibility. Such an attitude will usually spill over to other team members, creating an environment that is conducive to producing good results.

New Team Member Orientation

Since team building is an ongoing process, the team will want to establish procedures for orienting new team members who become involved after the initial development of the team. The procedures should include contacting the person on the telephone and describing the purpose and role of the transition team in the community. You should also spend some time with the new member, reviewing the team's plan and describing the team's current goals and progress to date. Also, be sure to spend time acquainting the new person with other team members, so that the new member doesn't feel like an outsider.

Enhancing Networking Capacity

Community transition teams have found that networking, which reaps so many benefits to students in transition, can be strengthened by acting in the following ways (Transition Assistance Project, 1997a):

- *Share your wealth,* including time, energy, skills, talents, and opportunities; good examples are the connecting activities that schools, colleges, employers, and agencies do.
- *Take time to care* by acknowledging those who reach out, and reach out yourself.
- *Lead by listening.* The heart of communication, listening promotes valuing; boosts sharing of ideas, dreams, and needs; and maximizes your capacity to put members' talents to their best use.
- *Commit to results* by building a lasting network, which requires investments of time, energy, and expertise.

SUMMARY

Team building is both the first phase of implementing a community transition team and an ongoing process that occurs throughout the life of the team. Although a set of standard procedures has been developed for establishing a team framework and identifying team members, each team develops its own special character in response to local geographical and political realities. Team membership is a fluid phenomenon, and procedures are required for orienting new members who join the team from time to time. It has often been said that the two golden rules of working with volunteers are:

- Ask them for their help, so they feel that they are needed; and
- Thank them for their help, so they feel that they are appreciated.

Undoubtedly, you can imagine many ways to help new team members (and old ones, for that matter!) feel that they are both needed and appreciated. The success of your team may well depend on your ability to do this well.

CHAPTER 3

Setting the Team Up for Success

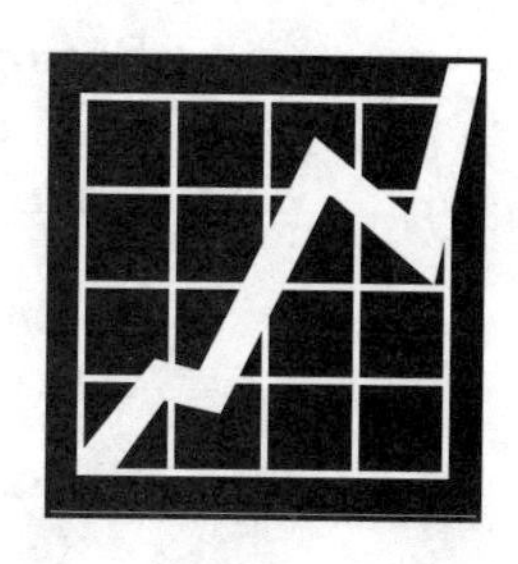

PLANNING MEETINGS

The initial meetings of the team can place it en route to productivity by using a few key strategies. This chapter shares some techniques that teams have found helpful in achieving efficient, effective operations.

Locations of Meetings

Numerous factors are helpful to review when determining where to hold meetings so that many persons will attend, particularly those who represent the community's key stakeholder groups. First, cultural, ethnic, economic, political, and geographic differences promote more separation than we might like in many communities. Hold the meetings at a place that invites all groups to participate, such as a community center or restaurant. Due to its institutional nature, it is risky to assume that the school will necessarily be perceived as a friendly place—no matter how friendly and connected the school staff try to be. The same perception may hold true for city hall or the bank, so ask a few questions and think through the implications when selecting the site. If the school is the only sensible meeting place, the gymnasium or library may represent more neutral territory than the administrative offices.

Second, select a site that is central to the geographical region covered by the team, to maximize attendance. A related strategy is to agree to rotate around the region so that all the geographical subgroups "host" a meeting, thereby increasing ownership of the team's activities. An advantage to rotating is that schools, employers, and adult agencies each have a chance to display physical features and even specific activities of their programs or operations.

Third, ensure physical accessibility of meeting sites, or risk sending the message that members with disabilities or other special needs are not really valued. This may mean nearby parking, availability of restrooms and beverages, whiteboards, sufficient ventilation, absence of chemicals, adequate lighting, space for movement, comfortable furniture, or other features in addition to ramps, elevators, door width, and more typical access markers.

Personal–Social Considerations for Meetings

Adults bring many issues to their shared activities. Common needs include thirst, hunger, and fatigue, so offering beverages, snacks (or even a meal), comfortable seating, and opportunity for periodic movement may be essential to drawing and keeping participants. Many adults are parents (often, in this case, of children with special needs), so skilled childcare may be a prerequisite for parents or guardians who are thinking about joining your group.

Sociopolitical considerations are also important in arranging meetings; every decision communicates a value to potential members that may help them decide whether to participate or not. Be sure to address the following issues.

- Do the meeting dates, times, and locations accommodate the most important stakeholder groups, particularly students, families, and employers?
- Have *multiple* members of potentially "marginalized" groups been invited (e.g., students, families, culturally or linguistically diverse citizens, gay or lesbian citizens, citizens of lower socioeconomic status), since greater numbers increase the likelihood of their voices being heard?
- Does the location disproportionately favor (or ignore) an individual, a group, or a management level?
- Have interpreters for the deaf and/or translators for those with language differences been provided? Even though participants may be capable of communicating at a basic level without support, such assistance increases understanding of the subtleties involved in sharing and decision making and may help someone decide whether to come or not.

The team can do a number of things to ensure that diverse groups feel invited to be equal partners in the planning process. Several suggestions proposed by Navarrete and White (1994) for increasing the multicultural competence of team members are included in Table 3.1.

TABLE 3.1

Strategies To Increase Team Members' Multicultural Competence

Strategy	Sample Activities
1. Provide opportunities for team members to learn about world views (of self, of others).	• Visit other sites. • Bring representatives of underrepresented groups to share their perceptions.
2. Provide opportunities for team members to learn about intercultural communication styles.	• Have "experts" share information. • Have members read and discuss article(s).
3. Encourage team members to learn as much as possible about their own cultures.	• Conduct focus groups. • Keep journals and conduct follow-up discussions.
4. Subscribe to resources that focus on multicultural issues and transition.	• Ask friends and colleagues about sources. • Check local libraries and agency offices.
5. Encourage team members to get involved in discussion groups that address diversity issues.	• Set up subgroups within the transition team. • Check electronic listserv groups.
6. Survey families in the community to gain feedback about the effectiveness of their child's services.	• Ask target questions during IEP meetings. • Conduct a written or telephone survey.
7. Incorporate concrete experiences with families from diverse backgrounds in teacher training programs.	• Begin a Families as Faculty project. • Set up family and student panels. • Require service learning assignments.

Note. Adapted from "School to Community Transition Planning: Factors To Consider When Working with Culturally Diverse Students and Families in Rural Settings," by L. A. Navarette and W. J. White, 1994, *Rural Special Education Quarterly, 13,* p. 54. Copyright 1994 by Rural Special Education Quarterly.

MEETING PROCEDURES

Holding Meetings That Are Worth Attending

Of course, one way to increase attendance by team members—and ultimately to increase the success of the team—is to hold meetings that are worth attending. The Transition Assistance Project (1996b) offers several guidelines for successful meetings.

- Set an agenda and stick to it.
- Ask members to help set the next agenda.
- Allot a certain amount of time per item, and get help staying on task.
- Set a specific day, time, and place for meetings at the beginning of each year.
- Establish ground rules for how the meetings will operate.
- Develop an orientation packet and a process for welcoming new members.
- Rely on a team approach to get work done; identify captains to lead each subcommittee to accomplish established goals.

Maximizing Voices in Initial Meetings

A variety of techniques can be used by teams to ensure that the voices of all individuals and groups are included. Following is a targeted list of suggestions.

1. At the first meeting, conduct an icebreaker activity that also relates to the meeting's purpose. For example, a "headhunter" activity asks participants to draw the silhouette of a head, divide the head into equal parts (2, 3, or 4), and write responses to your preplanned questions in each area. Appropriate questions might include a list of current life roles, the way(s) the person's current job was acquired, and the most critical outcomes for students after school. Participants then turn in their unnamed "heads," which are redistributed. Participants must search out the person whose "head" they hold by asking questions related to the responses. Each person then introduces their new acquaintance to the entire group, sharing whatever information the leader designates. This information can serve as an important record for initial goal statements or other data.
2. At the first meeting, ask all participants to share why they came—what are the burning issues that sparked their interest? Write their issues on a transparency using a projector, or on a whiteboard, chalkboard, or butcher paper, to validate what was said, create conceptual categories, and minimize duplicate discussions. These serve as important records of the meeting.
3. Use a cooperative processing structure (Carl, n.d.)—such as brainstorming, clarification, pros and cons, or another of your choice—to guarantee that every participant feels free to voice his or her thoughts.

Brainstorming Round

- One person at a time speaks, offering one item per turn.
- All members respond in turn, going around the table or group.
- No discussion or clarification is permitted.
- Each person must contribute an item or pass.
- A person who passes may respond on the next round unless the round is over.
- The round is over when all members have passed or time is called.

Clarification Round

- Speak in turn.
- Ask for clarification of one item per turn or pass.
- Take clarification only from the person who originally offered the item.
- End the round when all members have passed or time is called.

Pros and Cons

- Speak in turn, offering one statement of support on one item per turn.
- Make brief statements in support of an item.
- Don't repeat previous points; offer new reasons.
- Speak in support or pass.
- End the round when all members have passed or time is called.

4. Consider using the following cooperative voting structures (Carl, n.d.) to support decision making by voting or consensus.

Clear-Out Vote

- Members consider each item in turn.
- All vote at the same time.
- Open hand means retain; closed hand means eliminate.
- Item is retained or eliminated by a simple majority vote.
- Everyone votes on every item.

Weighted Vote

- Members consider each item in turn.
- Recorder counts and records votes.
- All members vote at same time by holding up 0, 1, 2, or 3 fingers.
- Top-scoring item(s) constitute the team's decision.

5. One threat to the members' "voices" may be a perception about competing forces. If you or the team have the opportunity, encourage related groups to meet independently, but also to be sure to represent themselves, both individually and as a group, in the team's discussions. An example of this would be a group of district-level transition specialists in the region, who meet regularly in order to do their work well. They may need to draw in other related groups who are represented in the community transition team, such as work-study coordinators, district administrators, or vocational rehabilitation counselors, from time to time. The transition specialists may function like one of the team's subcommittees in making major accomplishments in transition, even though they operate separately.

WEIGHING THE COMMITMENT TO CHANGE

Improving transition services and programs through the support of a community team, in concert with efforts at the student and school levels, works best when participating team members have shown an interest in change and a willingness to pursue change (Smith & Edelen-Smith, 1993). Halpern, Benz, and Lindstrom (1992) found that four guiding principles related to the change process serve as an important philosophical framework:

1. *Local control of implementation:* This is the real reason for creating the local community team.

2. *An evolutionary perspective on change:* Identify what's needed in order to achieve the outcomes needed in the community, and then create a plan.
3. *A focusing of change efforts on program capacity:* Simultaneously find out what students need through person-centered IEP planning, and combine that with building the system's ability to provide critical supports and options.
4. *Networking to connect the team's efforts:* Create ways to share ideas, strategies, opportunities, and resources.

Spending time evaluating at least a *core* group's commitment to change would be wise before wasting many people's time or an agency's money on setting up a community transition team. If some indication of support for change exists, then the team's activities themselves will help bring many others on board and exert the external pressure often needed to move bureaucracies to advance. The questionnaire in Figure 3.1 has been useful, through an interview process, to begin assessing a community's readiness for change and to identify staff development and support needs in preparation for developing a local team (Blalock, 1996). It is

District or Agency: ____________________ Date(s): ____________________

Contact Person: ____________________ Interviewer: ____________________

* *

How many residents are in your community?

How many students are in your school and/or district?

Roughly, what is the ethnic and spoken language makeup of your community?

How are those groups represented in district and community decisions?

Are you likely to be the person to take the lead in transition services in your area?

If not, who?

How is your district involving parents?

Would a translator help participation by parents?

What is working exceptionally well in your overall special education program?

What is not working so well?

Are the team members you have suggested strong in terms of energy, power to make decisions, and representativeness of your community?

What do you see as the greatest barriers to developing and improving your transition process?

Would people in your district see this team development as coming from the top down or from the bottom up, or both? What about people in your community?

How well does the school know the community, and vice versa (e.g., economy, cultural values, attitudes, etc.)?

Is the district superintendent supportive of school-to-careers transition programs?

What exists in your district to encourage teachers to make changes?

Are there any other details about your situation that would help in decision making?

FIGURE 3.1. Questions to assess district readiness for educational change.

just one more tool for setting the team up for success by analyzing strengths, gaps, and issues.

Finally, helping group members figure out the right questions to ask may be important, especially if transition ideology and programs are new for many. Some local teams have sent representative members (teachers, administrators, employers, and/or parents) to visit another site, perhaps even in another state, where the programs are further along. Support such as this can help a team quickly move light-years ahead, because many need to actually see the process work for students.

SUSTAINING THE MOMENTUM FOR CHANGE

The community transition team can *initiate* tremendous momentum during its first few months or year through the processes described so far and through those that will be described later: needs assessment and action planning. However, *maintaining* that power over the period of time needed to really make an impact is much harder. Our separate and combined experiences have taught us that some type of *external support structure* is needed to keep the momentum going.

Here are some examples. A regional transition coordinator hired by a rural cooperative or an area education agency helps do the initial team recruitment, facilitates the first few meetings, conducts and analyzes the needs assessment under the team's guidance, facilitates the action planning, and helps set up an evaluation system. This assumption of responsibility works well since teachers, administrators, rehabilitation counselors, and employers already have very full plates (just be sure that the team doesn't give away all its ownership). However, the initial achievements may not go very far, unless this coordinator or someone else from the agency also visits regularly, helps solve problems, serves as a liaison to break down interagency barriers, and seeks out critical resources and staff development options. This regular monitoring does several things: (a) It provides the accountability needed in systems to prompt all members to follow through; (b) it provides support at the needed times, which can make all the difference in a program's success; (c) it is typically founded upon a set of external expectations that school-to-work initiatives, systems change projects, or other state plans have targeted; (d) it provides visible, tangible validation for district and community efforts; (e) it greatly enhances networking capacity; and (f) it provides support for ongoing professional development in priority areas.

Many other entities also could accomplish this external support role. Some states have mandated state transition interagency councils who oversee the work of the community transition teams; they may even bring several teams together regularly for greater system impact. Other states have used their transition systems change project grants in this manner, and probably many of the school-to-work implementation grants will do the same. In some cases, other federal grant projects have funded the staff who provide the ongoing support. The source does not appear to be as important as the mere fact that it exists and that the people involved in transition activities know that their work is being examined and validated.

Several other mechanisms for strategizing for success are presented in this manual. *Developing a mission statement* for your group will help the team members concentrate on priorities rather than wasting time. The *needs assessment procedures* will provide critical data for identifying directions for change. *Evaluating, and then expanding upon, the team's accomplishments* will be essential for maximum effectiveness and sustainability of important practices. Taken as a package of approaches, these multiple facets of team development can create a powerful vehicle for systems change in transition at the local level.

DEVELOPING A MISSION STATEMENT FOR THE TEAM

A local community team typically can identify critical transition needs in their area in an initial 2- or 3-hour meeting. However, some states have found that developing a mission statement is a cornerstone for future activities and effectiveness. This section briefly describes the reasons for creating a mission statement and the process through which the team's mission statement can be developed in order to reflect and disseminate the group's shared vision.

Rationale

Carl (n.d.) suggested that mission statements should be:

- clear, jargon-free, and understandable;
- concise enough for everyone to remember and use; and
- compelling, powerful, and urgent

Mission statements that meet these criteria can be vital tools for inspiring and energizing the team as well as the broader community. A mission statement will help everyone understand where the group is going and how each member fits in. Additionally, it focuses the group's efforts and its accountability.

Procedures for Developing the Mission Statement

In Hawaii, Smith and Edelen-Smith (1993) found that teams needed about 16 hours, over the course of 2 months, to generate by consensus a precise vision or mission statement. Your team, like theirs, will need plenty of autonomy to identify its own direction. Otherwise, the members' excitement about and commitment to both team success and student outcomes will rapidly diminish.

The following steps are designed to help team members reach an agreement on a mission statement (adapted from Carl, n.d.).

1. Have each team member share his or her role on the team. What stakeholder group does he or she represent? Why is he or she there?
2. Have each team member share his or her perspectives, values, and beliefs regarding the transition process. For example, who should drive the decision-making process? What are his or her dreams about the transition process? What should students' outcomes be? Use the cooperative processing structures listed earlier in this chapter, or other techniques you know, to reach an agreement on a set of values and a vision.
3. Have each team member describe his or her agency's or organization's mission and how it seems to connect with the team's perceived mission. Zero in on the overlapping themes.
4. Have each team member describe the persons served by his or her organization or agency.
5. Have each team member outline potential personal or organizational resources that could be used to support the team's mission.

6. Using cooperative processing structures or other techniques, narrow down the shared purpose or goal of the group to one or two statements that answer the following questions:
   - On whose behalf are we acting?
   - What is our target achievement(s)?
   - What are the major means we will use to get there?

Referring frequently to the values, vision, and mission statements will help the group and its external support systems stay focused and energized in the future.

CHAPTER 4

Identifying the Community's Highest Priority Needs

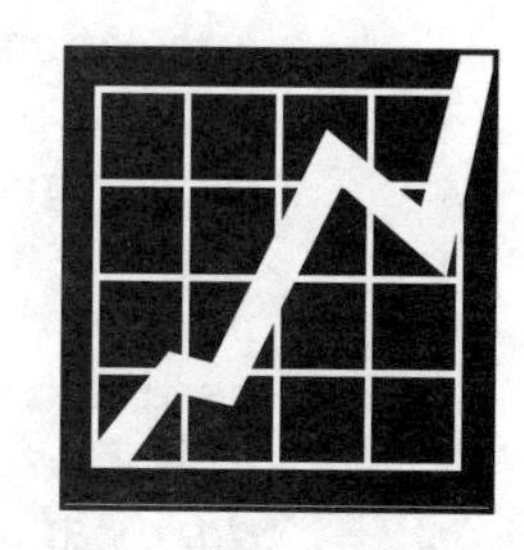

The overall intent of the needs assessment process is for teams to review carefully the current status of secondary special education, transition, and adult service programs and resources in their community. The needs assessment process addresses the overall question, "How are we, the school and the community, doing in our job to help students with disabilities prepare for a satisfactory life as young adults?" The answer to this basic question leads to a greater awareness of the program changes needed to achieve this broad goal.

During the needs assessment process, teams self-evaluate the status of secondary special education and transition services in their community. Based upon this self-evaluation, teams identify 3 to 5 areas to improve during the next year. Typically, the needs assessment phase is accomplished through two meetings, each lasting 1½ to 2 hours. During the first meeting, teams identify a finite list of 8 to 10 program improvement goals from the wide array of general issues in schools and communities that need to be addressed to improve transition services and outcomes for youth with disabilities. During the second meeting, teams select 3 to 5 top-priority areas that they will address during the next year.

Three characteristics of the needs assessment process are particularly important. First, the approach is based entirely on *self-evaluation,* rather than third-party evaluation. Second, the process of needs assessment is *locally referenced.* In other words, it assumes that program needs will vary from community to community. Third, the needs assessment process provides a *foundation* for subsequent program planning. The result of this self-evaluation approach is information specifically relevant to the team's own community, and with direct implications for completing the subsequent phases of the transition team process: program planning, program implementation, and program evaluation.

NEEDS ASSESSMENT PROCEDURES

The needs assessment process includes two major components: (a) identify program improvement goals and (b) select 3 to 5 top-priority goals. Each of these components is usually completed in the context of a team meeting.

Identify 8 to 10 Program Improvement Goals

The purpose of this first component of the needs assessment process is to help team members identify a finite list of program improvement goals. This is not as easy as it may seem. In most communities, there are many aspects of secondary school curricula and programs, transition services, and adult agency and community resources that *could* be improved to better serve youth with disabilities and their families. Moreover, there are many perspectives about which aspects of the school and community are most in need of improvement, and many of these perspectives will be represented on the team (e.g., parents, students and/or school leavers, school and adult agency staff, and community representatives). The challenge is to identify a concrete, finite, feasible list of program improvement goals that incorporates the perspectives of these various stakeholders. Two approaches have been used successfully to help team members identify and achieve consensus on a list of important program improvement goals for their community: a *program standards* approach and a *nominal group process* approach.

Program Standards Approach to Identifying Improvement Goals

In the program standards approach to goal identification, team members use a "needs assessment instrument" to rate existing program improvement goal statements. Typically, in this approach, needs assessment standards represent a series of broadly stated goals for program improvement efforts. The scope of the standards should be broad enough to represent the complexity of the school and adult services systems but also specific enough to serve as the foundation for a concrete action plan. One such instrument (Halpern, Lindstrom, Benz, & Rothstrom, 1991), used by local teams in Oregon and other states associated with the Community Transition Team Model, is included in Appendix C. In this particular instrument, 38 standards are organized under 6 major categories, including: (a) curriculum and instruction, (b) mainstreaming and coordination, (c) transition services, (d) documentation, (e) administrative support, and (f) adult services and community resources. A rating process is built into the instrument that calls for each standard to be rated along two dimensions: the importance (value) of the standard for creating comprehensive, high-quality secondary and transition services, and the extent to which the standard is already being met in the community (current status).

If the team chooses this approach to identifying program improvement goals, use the instrument in Appendix C or another similar instrument to complete the following activities. First, have team members rate each standard for its value (importance in providing quality transition services) and current status (extent to which it is already achieved). Generally, it is desirable to have team members complete the needs assessment instrument in a meeting since it sets the context for self-evaluation by having an initial discussion about the program improvement areas and the rating concepts, and by answering team members' questions about the process. All team members should complete the value scale for each item; everyone should have an opinion about whether or not a particular item needs to be addressed. Only those who are familiar with the current status of a standard may want to complete the current status scale. By summing the value and current status ratings, each standard will receive a score. The lower the score, the less priority is ascribed to a given standard for the community transition team to address at the present time. A higher score indicates an important standard that is not yet completely achieved.

Second, the team leader or a subgroup of team members should summarize the individual ratings and rank order the standards based on the sum (or average) of the ratings of all team members. Rank ordering the standards will allow the team to identify the top 8 to 10 goals that will become the focus of the next component of the needs assessment process. Typically, the summing or averaging of team members' ratings occurs between the initial team meeting, where team members rated the goal statements, and the second team meeting in which team members select the 3 to 5 top-priority goals for the next year.

Nominal Group Process Approach to Identifying Improvement Goals

In the nominal group process approach to goal identification, team members use a structured process first to identify possible areas of improvement and then to rank them to identify the 8 to 10 goal areas that should be the general focus of the team's activities for the next year. The nominal group procedures described in this section are based on the program planning approach developed by Delbecq, Van de Ven, and Gustafson (1975). The nominal group process approach offers several advantages over more typical, "free-flowing" brainstorming approaches. First, research conducted by Delbecq and others has shown the nominal group process to be far superior to group brainstorming approaches in terms of the number of relevant, unique, and quality ideas generated. Second, nominal group approaches, although highly structured, actually facilitate higher levels of creativity among group members. Finally, in heterogeneous groups, such as a transition team, nominal group processes encourage greater participation by all members and reduce the likelihood that "dominant personality types" will influence the nature and focus of the discussion.

If the team chooses the nominal group process approach to identify program improvement goals, use the procedures outlined in Table 4.1 to help team members create a list of 8 to 10 goals. The process presented in Table 4.1 assumes that the team has more than 12 members during the needs assessment phase, and describes a set of steps involving subgroups of members in order to encourage greater participation by all team members. If the team has 10 or fewer members, complete the structured discussion process as an entire team. This can be done by using the same general process described in Table 4.1 without the subgroup activities. Like the program standards approach described earlier, the outcome of the nominal group process approach should be 8 to10 program improvement goals that the entire team has discussed and agreed (voted on) are important to enhancing the capacity of schools and communities to serve the transition needs of youth with disabilities and their families.

Select 3 to 5 Top-Priority Goals

Regardless of which approach to goal identification was used, at this point in the needs assessment process, the team will have identified 8 to 10 goal areas that are in need of improvement. The team cannot address all of these goals in one year, of course. The purpose of this step in the needs assessment process is to identify a smaller number of goals that will structure the team's annual plan during the upcoming year. Teams accomplish this process in a goal setting meeting, in which the entire set of 8 to 10 goals is discussed by team members to identify a subset of 3 to 5 top-priority goals. Use the following three steps to identify the team's highest priority goals.

1. Engage team members in a structured discussion of each of the 8 to 10 goals using the major selection factors of *support, feasibility,* and *impact.* Underlying the *support* factor is the critical importance of selecting goals that will encourage the interest and involvement of a majority of team members, whether they represent parental interests, schools, adult service agencies, or the community in general. Attending to the issue of *feasibility* will increase the likelihood that the team will successfully complete the selected goals. Thinking about the desired *impact* of the goals will help identify those goals that hold the greatest immediate potential for affecting the lives of adolescents and young adults with disabilities in the community. Discussing the entire set

TABLE 4.1

Summary of Steps Involved in the Nominal Group Process

1. Depending upon the size of the team, divide the team into subgroups of 6 to 8 members each, ensuring as much as possible that each subgroup remains representative of the team overall (e.g., do not have all school staff in one subgroup and all parents in another subgroup). This encourages greater variability in the goals identified by each subgroup. Ask one member from each subgroup to serve as a facilitator.
2. Provide each team member with paper or 3 × 5 cards. Instruct them to "List the things you would like to see improved in the schools or in the community in order to help youth transition successfully from school to the community. As best you can, try to write these things as positive goal statements that we could work on as a team (e.g., 'provide students with more job experience in high school' or 'provide families with more information about community resources')." Instruct team members that they are to do this step independently and without speaking to other team members in their group. Give them 20 to 30 minutes to complete this step.
3. At the end of the allotted time, provide each subgroup with some large poster paper, marking pens, and masking tape. Ask the subgroup facilitator to serve as recorder for his or her group. Within each subgroup, ask team members, *one at a time,* to give one goal statement from the list of goals they have created. As each team member reports on his or her goal, the facilitator records the goal on the large poster paper exactly as the team member reports it. Continue this round-robin process of having one team member report one goal until all team members have reported all the goals they have created. If team members have created similar goals these may be designated by checkmarks rather than writing out similar goals. Take only as much time as is minimally necessary to record each member's goals.
4. After all goals are recorded, give each subgroup 20 to 30 minutes to discuss, clarify, and elaborate on the entire list of goals they have created. At the end of the 20 to 30 minutes, give the subgroup members 3 × 5 cards and ask them to vote privately on the 5 goals they feel are most crucial to address. Give the subgroups 10 minutes to complete this voting activity. Have subgroup facilitators collect the voting cards and record (with help if necessary) the votes of the subgroup directly on the paper next to the relevant goals. Give subgroup members a break while the votes are being tallied and recorded.
5. Assemble the work of the subgroups and bring all team members back together. Give each subgroup 5 to 7 minutes to report on the top 5 goals that emerged from their identification, discussion, and voting activities. The specific number of goals that you ask subgroups to report on will depend on the number of subgroups. The outcome of this reporting process should be approximately 12 to 15 goal statements that become the focal point for discussion and voting by the entire team.
6. Give the entire team 20 to 30 minutes to discuss, clarify, and elaborate on the combined list of 12 to 15 goals that have now emerged from the work of the subgroups. Keep the group focused on understanding the purpose and intent of the goal statements. Sometimes, during these discussions, team members will drift into generating solutions to the problems that appear on the list as a way of deciding whether a goal is important or worth pursuing.
7. At the end of the 20 to 30 minutes, give the group members 3 × 5 cards and ask them to vote privately on the 5 goals they feel are most crucial to address. Give the group 10 minutes to complete this voting activity. After the voting is complete, collect the voting cards and set the time and location for the next needs assessment meeting in which team members will review the results of the voting and select 3 to 5 top-priority goals to address in the upcoming year.

of 8 to 10 goals from the perspective of these three selection criteria can help create a common frame of reference for team members to use in selecting the highest priority goals for the upcoming year. One note of caution: Allow for discussion, but keep the group focused on the task of prioritizing goals based on the selection criteria. Past experience has shown that during this part of the meeting some team members can drift into problem-solving discussions rather than focusing on the selection of goals.

2. Select the top goals by having each team member vote for his or her top 3 priorities. Use an overhead transparency or poster paper to record team members' votes. Add the total points to determine the top 3 to 5 goals for the entire team.
3. Once the top 3 to 5 goals have been identified, obtain consensus on these top goals. Ask, "Is there anyone who *can't* live with these goals for the next year?" Allow discussion until team members agree that 3 to 5 selected goals are the most important ones for the team to address over the next year.

SUMMARY

Needs assessment is the true beginning of building a functional community transition team, since it provides both a *set of goals* for focusing team efforts and a *process* for selecting the set of goals. The discussions that emerge during this stage are very important for solidifying relationships among team members. If these discussions go well, a common commitment to the goals of the plan will emerge, and a sense of collaboration and respect will grow among team members.

The careful structuring of this process provides a way to both examine the array of possible needs in a comprehensive manner and select the most important needs to be addressed at a given point in time. The outcome of the needs assessment process will leave the team poised for action. The next phase of the community transition team process, program planning, provides a way of harnessing this motivation into a concrete set of useful activities designed to achieve the selected goals.

CHAPTER 5

Developing an Effective Plan of Action

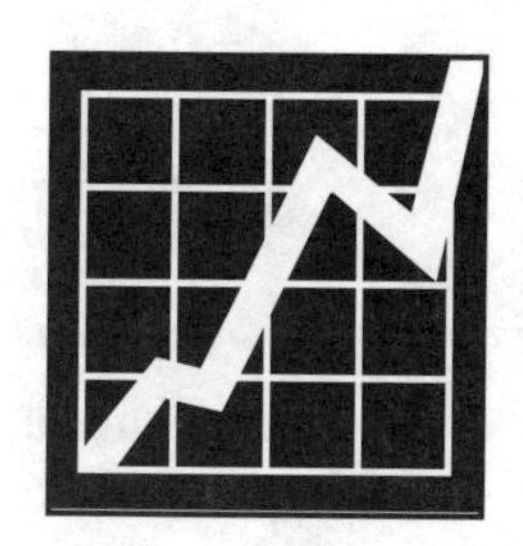

The next phase of the community transition team process is *action planning.* Starting with the 3 to 5 top-priority goals identified in the needs assessment phase, the team will move through a series of planning steps, enabling it to develop those broad goal statements into a working plan. The plan will spell out the specific objectives and tasks to be accomplished over the year, who will do the work, and the timelines for completion.

The action planning phase obviously is very important, since it provides the work plan for making the changes in local community services and resources that are needed to improve the school experiences and post-school outcomes of young people with disabilities. The system being proposed is a familiar "management-by-objectives" approach. There are several basic characteristics of this planning approach, including:

- The process is structured through identification of "action-oriented" goals and objectives;
- A task analysis and timelines are developed for each objective; and
- Resources are identified for implementing the set of tasks specified for accomplishing each objective in the plan.

The action planning procedures presented here follow this approach fairly closely. The basic intent is to provide a method of helping team members identify clearly what needs to be done and *how* it will be accomplished. The planning process also provides team members, who represent various agencies and perspectives, with an opportunity to explore ways of collaborating with one another while working toward a common goal. The commitments that emerge from this process have the potential of improving the basic structure of service delivery in local communities including a willingness to collaborate. Many team members we have worked with over the years have commented on this outcome as a major benefit of their participation on the transition team.

PROCEDURES FOR DEVELOPING AN ANNUAL ACTION PLAN

Transition teams typically develop their first annual plan during a day-long action planning workshop. This workshop is followed by a meeting of the entire team to review and finalize the plan. This format has proven to be the most efficient use of time for team members. A sample agenda for a day-long planning workshop and follow-up meeting is presented in Table 5.1.

Occasionally, teams have used a series of three, half-day meetings to develop their first annual plan. Under this format, teams typically have completed all activities up through the first planning session during the first half-day meeting,

TABLE 5.1

Sample Agenda for Planning Workshop and Follow-Up Meeting

Planning Workshop 8:30 A.M.–4:00 P.M.	
8:30 A.M.	**Introductions (if new members are present)**
9:00 A.M.	**Overview of the Planning Workshop** —Review the transition team purpose and process. —Give an overview of the planning process.
9:30 A.M.	**Review of the Top-Priority Goals Selected by the Team** —Present the top-priority goals. —Review key discussion points.
10:00 A.M.	**Break**
10:15 A.M.	**First Planning Session: Identify Objectives for Each Goal** —Identify a list of possible objectives. —Select the objective(s) for each goal.
12:00 P.M.	**Lunch**
1:00 P.M.	**Second Planning Session: Develop Each Objective** —Identify tasks and timelines for the first objective. —Select a workgroup for each remaining objective. —Identify tasks and timelines for each remaining objective. —Reconvene as a group and review all objectives. —Identify a time and place for the next team planning meeting.
4:00 P.M.	**Adjourn**
Follow-up Planning Meeting 4:00 P.M.–6:30 P.M.	
4:00 P.M.	**Review and Complete Plan** —Review the objectives, tasks, and timelines for each goal. —Review the task/time calendar and adjust the plan as needed. —Identify persons and resources for each objective.
5:30 P.M.	**Discussion Strategies for Implementing the Plan** —Establish subcommittees and basic operational procedures. —Set a time and place for next meeting.
6:30 P.M.	**Adjourn Meeting**

and the second planning session then becomes the focus of the second half-day meeting. The follow-up planning meeting, of course, remains unchanged regardless of which format is used. Team members should determine which format will work best for their circumstances, and together develop an appropriate agenda. This chapter will describe the action planning process using the planning workshop format presented in Table 5.1.

Planning Workshop Activities

Review the Top-Priority Goals

At the beginning of the program planning workshop, it is useful to review the goals selected at the end of the needs assessment meeting. This provides a good introduction to the purpose of the workshop, and it also allows the team to reaffirm the decisions that have been made. At this point in the process, if any new members have joined your team for the first time, a quick review also provides them with a way of becoming acquainted with the activities they have missed.

Identify One or More Objectives for Each Goal

To identify objectives, use the nominal group process described in the previous chapter on needs assessment. Depending on how many team members are present, the nominal group procedures can be used in subgroups or with the entire team. Follow the same general process used during the needs assessment phase. For each goal, ask team (or subgroup) members to "List specific objectives that you would like to see the team work on to accomplish this goal." To ensure that all team members have a common frame of reference on how to write an objective, write the following "Hints for Writing a Good Objective" on a large piece of paper and post it for all to see.

Hints for Writing a Good Objective

- It clearly relates to the goal being addressed.
- It is written in the form of a "what will be done" to address the goal statement, such as:

  A study will be conducted to . . .
  A curriculum will be developed to . . .
  Training will be provided to . . .
- It will result in a measurable, observable outcome.
- It is narrow enough in scope to be achievable within 1 to 2 years.

Have team (or subgroup) members share their objectives in the same round-robin manner used during needs assessment, discuss the objectives, and then vote on the highest priority objectives for the next year. The outcome of this process should be several rank-ordered objectives for each of the team's top-priority goals.

The number and type of objectives for each goal is a decision that is left entirely to the discretion of the team. It is recommended, however, that the total number of chosen objectives be small in order to ensure that your team is able to manage the workload without overburdening the members. In the enthusiasm of the moment, a typical pitfall is for teams to attempt far more than is realistic, which soon results in frustration as deadlines come and go and the objectives have yet to be accomplished.

One note of caution regarding the final set of objectives. It is important that the final set includes one or more objectives that are of interest to each individual team member. In the excitement of identifying objectives and creating meaningful action plans, it is easy to create a final set of objectives that is unidimensional (e.g., all objectives relate to developing new curricula or programs within the school). This can discourage the participation of parents or community members (e.g., employers) who may have other interests or who may feel they have nothing meaningful to contribute to the accomplishment of the plan.

If the team is following the format of a day-long planning workshop, the first planning session will now be done, and the team will be ready to break for lunch. If the team is using the format of half-day planning meetings, at this point, make sure all team members have the date, time, and location of the second planning meeting on their calendars. Regardless of which format is being used, when team members return they will be focusing on developing each selected objective into a specific action plan with tasks and timelines.

Develop Tasks and Timelines for Each Objective

Once a set of objectives has been identified for addressing the team's high priority goals, team members must develop tasks and timelines for each selected objective. Depending upon the number of team members present, and the number of selected objectives, decide whether to develop tasks and timelines in subgroups or as an entire team. The general rule here is to use an approach that will complete this step as efficiently as possible *and* that will maximize the participation of all team members. It is important to "demystify" the task analysis concept and help all team members feel they can create a set of "logical steps to go from point A to point B."

Once tasks and timelines have been created for each objective, team members should review the proposed task analysis for each objective to determine whether or not the sequence of tasks is a good work plan for the team. Engage team members in a discussion of the task analysis "as a whole." Is there a logical starting point for the objective? Does the sequence of tasks make sense, or are there critical steps missing in the identified sequence? Does the identified set of tasks allow the team to achieve the outcome intended for this objective? Revise the task analysis and timelines for each objective based on the outcomes of this discussion. Review the final task analysis for each objective with the entire team to obtain consensus and to bring the meeting to an end.

At this point, the basic framework for the team's annual action plan has been completed, and you are ready to schedule the date, time, and location of the follow-up planning meeting. If your experiences are like those of the many teams we have worked with over the years, this will have been hard work and team members will be exhausted. Congratulate each other for your efforts!

Several "clerical" tasks must now be completed in order to prepare materials for the follow-up planning meeting. First, the goals, objectives, and task analyses must be typed into the form of a draft annual plan that can be reviewed by team members. A suggested format for the draft annual plan is provided in Appendix D. Second, create a "task/time calendar" that organizes tasks across objectives by month. The task/time calendar is a useful way to help team members review the work scope of the entire plan by calendar month. Creating the task/time calendar is a relatively simple matter if the draft annual plan is developed on a computer with a standard word processing program. A sample task/time calendar is included in Appendix E.

Follow-Up Planning Meeting

The follow-up planning meeting is the link between the program planning and program implementation phases. During this meeting, the team finalizes the annual action plan and establishes the operational structure and procedures that will be used to implement the plan during the next year. Information on operational structure and procedures will be presented in the next chapter.

Review the Draft Annual Plan

To start the review process, distribute copies of the draft annual plan and the task/time calendar to team members and give them a few minutes to review each document. Begin with a discussion of the draft annual plan. The process of review involves three considerations: (a) whether or not the task analysis for each selected objective is adequate; (b) whether or not the calendar of monthly events is reasonable; and (c) whether or not the plan is overly ambitious.

Reviewing the task analysis for each selected objective is done in order to accommodate any "second thoughts" that team members might have about the most efficient way to accomplish the objective. Although past experience suggests that most teams do not make many changes in this area, providing team members with an *opportunity* to do so is an important part of the total planning process.

The team should also examine the reasonableness of the workload through their review of the task/time calendar and make any necessary adjustments. For example, if the team has inadvertently scheduled eight tasks to be completed in January and none for February, the necessary adjustments can then be made. The final calendar should be a reasonable one, which takes into account everyone's busy schedule.

The examination of the total calendar may lead to a consequence other than simply rearranging the proposed timelines. The team may decide that the total plan is too ambitious, and that it is prudent to eliminate or postpone one or more objectives. *This is not something to feel ashamed about!* During the early stages of planning, people often get caught up in the process and behave in a "let's do it all" manner. The more sober reflections of "the day after," however, may be more realistic. It is much better to do a few things well than to do many things poorly. This does not mean that ambitious plans are always out of the question. Some teams with which we have worked have adequately handled as many as 10 objectives within a single year. Other teams have struggled to complete a single objective. At this point in the process, you want to help your team to be realistic, biting off only what it is able to chew and digest. A successful outcome is much more important than an ambitious plan.

Identify Persons and Resources for Each Objective

Once team members have affirmed or revised and finalized the work scope, the next step is to identify the team members and other resources needed to accomplish each objective. Most teams organize their members into subcommittees to work on individual objectives. (Examples of how teams have developed subcommittees are presented in the next chapter.) During this step of the planning process, team members volunteer to work on one or more specific objectives. Team members also identify other resources needed to accomplish each objective. These resources may include personnel time other than that being volunteered by team members (e.g., some clerical support hours), a place to hold meetings, travel reimbursements, and/or a variety of materials and supplies needed to accomplish the adopted objectives.

Summarize All Information into a Final Annual Plan

The last step in the program planning process is to finalize the plan. After the team has completed its review of the draft annual plan and has identified persons and resources to implement the plan, it is ready to produce a final annual plan. This is simply a matter of incorporating the final revisions into the draft annual plan and the task/time calendar. Again, this revision process is greatly expedited if the drafts have been produced and saved through a computer word processing program. Together, the revised annual plan and task/time calendar become the framework for guiding the team's activities during the timeframe the plan is being implemented. The sample task/time calendar included in Appendix E includes a column to check when individual tasks have been completed in order to track progress within individual objectives.

If the team is interested in producing a final annual plan that can be disseminated to other interested stakeholders, it is suggested that three elements be added to the basic framework to create a self-contained, professional-looking product: (a) a face page (perhaps with a graphic) that clearly identifies the name and location of the community transition team, (b) a list of names and contact information for all team members, and (c) a copy of the team's mission statement.

SUMMARY

The outcome of the program planning phase is a thoughtfully constructed, written plan that lays out a set of objectives and tasks for addressing high-priority program improvement goals over the course of a year. Although a specific structure for developing the plan has been proposed here, the specific and unique content of the plan is left totally to the discretion of each individual team. This acknowledges that the transition team is in the best position to determine the most appropriate ways of improving programs and services in its local community. The standard format, however, facilitates the program planning process, provides a good foundation for evaluation, and eases the task of sharing information with other communities in the state that use community transition teams to improve secondary special education and transition programs.

CHAPTER 6
Implementing the Action Plan

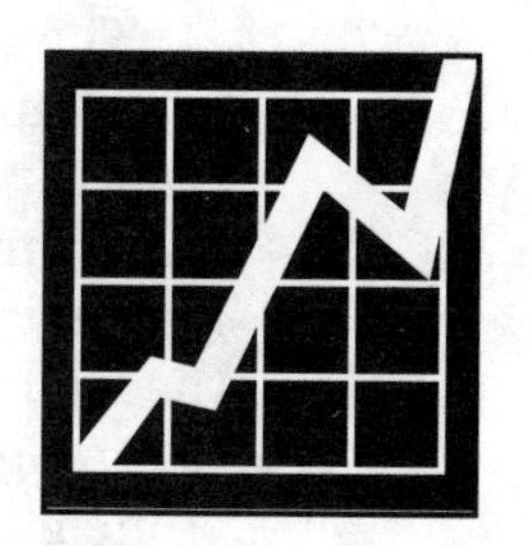

The next phase of the community transition team process is *program implementation.* During this phase, transition teams determine a structure for actually accomplishing the work specified in their annual plans, and then they set about the task of completing this work. Most teams choose to distribute the workload by breaking into subcommittees to address each objective in the annual plan, taking into consideration team members' areas of interest. The team leader supports this work by attending to logistics, monitoring the timely implementation of tasks, troubleshooting problems as they arise, and keeping the team motivated. Many teams find that additional resources are required, beyond what was specified in the annual plan, to implement certain objectives. The challenge then becomes one of identifying and securing the additional resources needed in order to complete these objectives, or modifying the objectives. Finally, an important activity during program implementation is networking with other community transition teams. Networking is defined as communication in the form of telephone contact, written correspondence, or meetings for the purposes of sharing information and materials and providing mutual support to one another.

The essence of the program implementation phase is the specification and employment of a set of procedures for encouraging and supporting a group of volunteers to accomplish the work of the team's annual plan. It is important to attend constantly to this essential reality, that transition teams are composed of volunteers. This means, of course, that each team member's own personal priorities will often compete with the team's priorities, which were negotiated during the euphoria of a planning workshop. When the reality of each person's personal and professional life sets in, it will be important to provide teams with a substantial amount of structure, guidance, and support to keep people involved with and focused upon their commitments to the objectives and tasks specified in the team's annual plan.

The team leader is the key person who is called upon to provide this support. In most instances, the team leader is also a volunteer. This reality must carefully be considered when developing a plan for program implementation. The team will be faced with the question of whether to develop an implementation style that fits the needs of a given leader or, alternatively, to develop a style that fits the team and then select a leader who is willing to act according to the team's desires. Although the latter alternative would seem to be desirable for the long-term stability of a team, there may be situations in which a strong leader, with his or her unique style, is more needed than a desired style for which no strong leader exists. The team will have to struggle with this issue as its implementation approach is developed and, perhaps, revised several times to take advantage of changing opportunities for leadership.

The procedures suggested in this chapter for program implementation have been found to work quite well for most teams. The presence of a strong team leader, however, is a clear and definite underlying assumption. Because of the central importance of the team leader, some teams may want to consider alternative implementation structures to the ones presented here, if they are needed in order to tap the leadership potential available in their community. If the choice ever boils down to strong team leadership versus the procedures for implementation that are recommended in this manual, you should definitely alter these suggested procedures to fit the needs of local leadership.

PROCEDURES FOR PROGRAM IMPLEMENTATION

There are four major components of program implementation: (a) Determine a team structure for accomplishing the plan, (b) establish the role of the team leader during program implementation, (c) identify and secure resources that are needed beyond those specified in the plan, and (d) network with other transition teams.

Determine a Team Structure for Accomplishing the Plan

Establishing a team structure is the critical beginning of program implementation. As with team building, decisions made during this step will determine how well teams are able to accomplish the tasks that they have undertaken. It is crucial to develop a team structure that will allow the team to proceed with its work in a timely manner without causing "burnout" among its members. Several possible ways to organize the team are suggested later in this chapter.

Establish Meeting Procedures

Although the major work of a transition team is usually done in subcommittees, the team should also meet regularly as a full team. Such meetings should occur no less than quarterly and no more than monthly. A meeting of the full transition team will serve three purposes:

1. to maintain a sense of cohesiveness among team members;
2. to facilitate communication regarding the implementation of the work plan; and
3. to provide support and feedback to the individuals or subcommittees who are actually doing the work.

A sense of cohesiveness among team members is important in light of the workload to be addressed and the commitment required to participate on the team. The opportunity to meet on a regular basis provides the necessary contact and communication among members to maintain commitment, avoid fragmentation of the group, and keep sight of the "big picture."

Meeting regularly as an entire team also enables members to remain informed about the specific tasks assigned to the subcommittees. This is accomplished by reserving agenda time during each meeting for subcommittee or individual progress reports. This type of structure also assists the team in remaining on task with the specified timelines for the plan or in making decisions on necessary changes in the plan. Finally, regularly scheduled full team meetings enable team members to use each other as resources for information. For example, a team member may know of additional resources for producing a videotape that were unknown to the committee charged with that activity.

Once the team has decided on the amount of work that it wants to undertake, establish and follow regular meeting procedures to facilitate the work of the team. Suggested procedures include a written agenda that is distributed to members prior to each meeting, an annual calendar of meeting times to allow people ample time to include this in their schedules, an appointed person (usually the team leader) to run the meeting and help people remain on task, and a person to take minutes.

The team may also find it helpful to leave each meeting with a fairly clear set of assignments describing what each team member should do in preparation for the next meeting. A reminder telephone call the day before the next meeting is scheduled may increase attendance. When scheduling meetings, the team should discuss the location to ensure that the selected site is convenient and agreeable for all members.

Some teams have found it useful and convenient to establish a very consistent schedule of meetings throughout the year. For example, the team may decide to meet the third Tuesday of every month between 3:30 and 5:00 P.M. at the school administration building. Teams that have adopted this approach claim that the "regularity" of transition team meetings helps ensure that members will keep them a high priority as they fill out their personal and professional calendars.

Establish Subcommittees

The number and types of subcommittees that the team chooses to adopt, along with the composition of each subcommittee, will relate directly to the content of the annual action plan and the interests of team members. Some teams choose to break into groups based on single objectives, such as "developing a transition manual," while others prefer to organize themselves by major areas such as curriculum development, administrative support, or adult services. Regardless of the approach taken, there are four important considerations in determining who will serve on subcommittees: leadership, representation, time commitment, and coordination with other related initiatives.

Leadership

A strong leader for each subcommittee is essential to accomplishing the work in a timely manner. Each subcommittee needs a leader to keep the group on task, to identify and troubleshoot problems with the work plan, and to manage the logistics for the group. In essence, this person serves as a team leader for the smaller group. This person may also be responsible for keeping the larger group informed of subcommittee progress.

Representation

A second consideration in subcommittee composition is representation. Each subcommittee should consist of members who, in addition to having an interest in the subcommittee's work, have the knowledge and expertise to carry out the work plan *and* who can bring a variety of perspectives to the group. For example, a subcommittee charged with developing or adopting a social skills curriculum for students with disabilities should include educators, adult service providers, parents, and students who are aware of the issues.

Time Commitment

The third consideration in determining a subcommittee structure is time commitment. When volunteering to serve on one or more subcommittees, team members should be realistic about the amount of time required to do the job well, and they should only make commitments that are possible to honor. Team members should use the task analysis for each objective to help them determine the feasibility of their individual assignments.

Coordination with Other Related Initiatives

The fourth and final consideration in determining a subcommittee structure (and, perhaps, general structure) is coordination with other related initiatives. Most teams find themselves having to respond simultaneously to several initiatives in addition to transition, such as supported employment, student retention, and early intervention. The problems are obvious: Given a limited number of potential team members in a community, the demand to address several major issues can quickly lead to burnout. Teams decide how to manage these issues when determining a team structure. One possible solution is to assign a subcommittee to any initiatives that are closely related to transition. A second possibility is to assign one or more transition team representatives to other existing councils. The representatives could then serve as a liaison between the two groups. In the latter situation, transition team representatives should take this added responsibility into account when deciding on which subcommittees to serve.

Examples of Team Structure

Figures 6.1 and 6.2 show two very different examples of organizational structures that were adopted by transition teams. The first example (Figure 6.1) is from a team in a very rural area. The team members represent several communities, which are spread out geographically. This team developed a model that includes a core team, as well as community clusters that report to the main team. Figure 6.1 displays the team's representative members, geographical composition, administrative structure, and team subcommittees. Figure 6.2 is an example of a more centralized team, with subcommittees structured around objectives from the annual

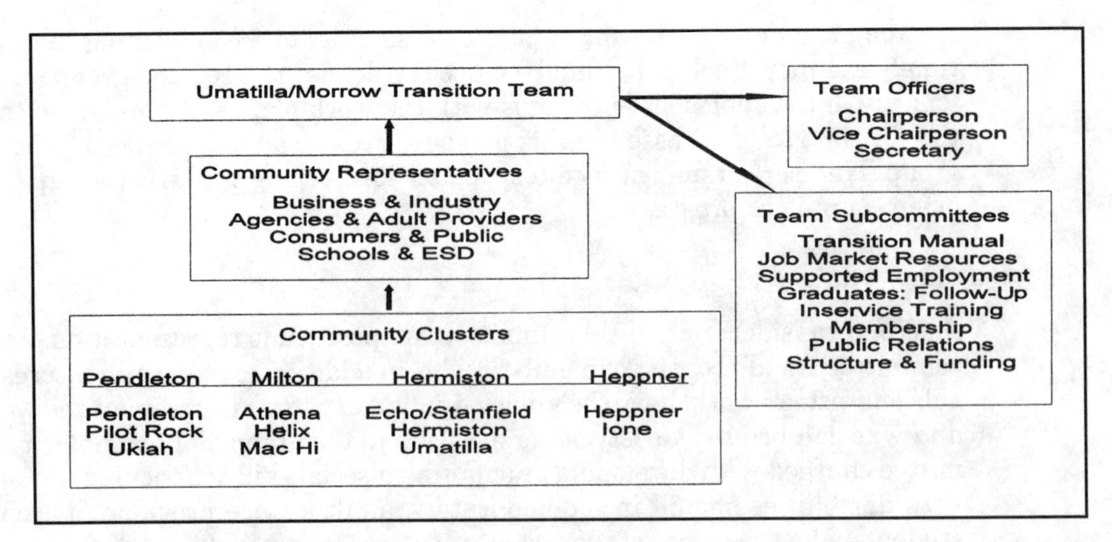

FIGURE 6.1. Sample organization chart for a rural community transition team.

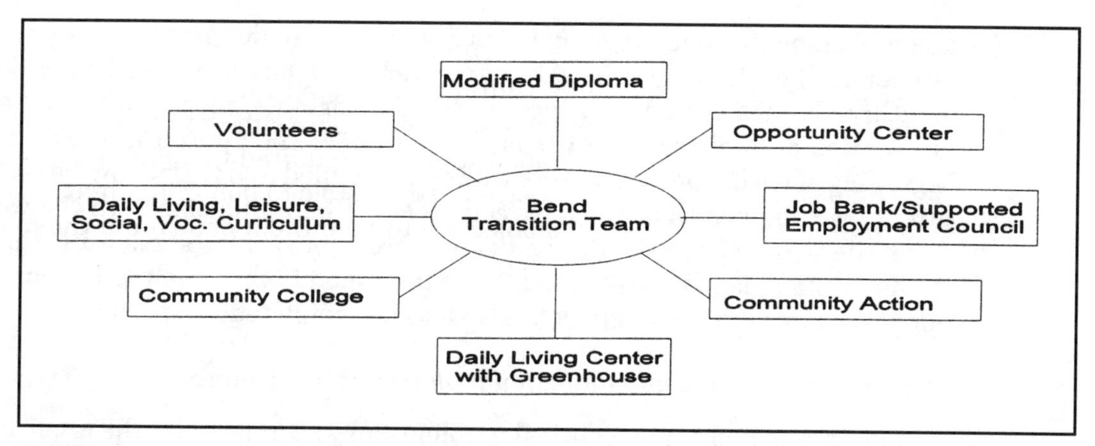

FIGURE 6.2. Sample organizational chart for centralized community transition team.

plan. Once your team has decided on a structure for the purpose of program implementation, it may be helpful to develop an organizational chart, such as the ones in these examples.

Establish the Role of the Team Leader

After clarifying the team structure for program implementation, it is also important to clarify the role of the team leader. The roles and responsibilities that the transition team leader may assume in whole or in part include: (a) Organize and guide implementation of the work plan; (b) identify and solve problems with the work plan; (c) identify and solve interpersonal and political problems encountered by the team; and (d) represent the team to agencies, consumers, and the general public.

The team may decide that its leader should assume full responsibility for certain roles and activities, or that several of these roles and activities should be shared between the team leader and other team members. Some leaders have chosen to appoint a "co-leader" who assumes some of the roles of the team leader. Since team leadership is the backbone of the entire process, as discussed above, this determination of the team leader's responsibilities is a crucial part of the process.

Organize and Guide Implementation of the Work Plan

The team leader (or co-leader) should organize the overall work plan for the team in several ways. First, the team leader should continue to oversee the logistics of team meetings, including reminding members of upcoming meetings, preparing and distributing the meeting agendas and minutes from the previous meeting, and acting as meeting leader. Second, the team leader should make sure that each meeting agenda includes updates or progress reports from all subcommittees or individuals working on various objectives or aspects of the plan. The team leader should monitor work assignments and deadlines, making sure that these tasks and timelines are clear and still manageable for team members. Finally, a year-long calendar of full committee meetings should be distributed early in the year to provide members with ample notice of where and when to attend meetings.

Identify and Solve Problems with the Work Plan

A second role assumed by team leaders (or co-leaders) is to identify and solve problems with the work plan. This entails remaining aware of tasks, timelines, and accomplishments on an ongoing basis in order to predict problems and to address problems when they do arise. One approach that has been used is to develop a monthly file card system in which each task, person(s) responsible, and deadline are written on a file card that is organized under the appropriate month. At the beginning of each month, the file cards can be pulled and tasks may be checked off throughout the month as they are completed. When problems with the work plan arise, the team leader should facilitate a problem-solving session in which team members offer suggestions to modify the task, modify the timeline, or acquire additional resources that will allow the task to be completed as specified.

Identify and Solve Interpersonal and Political Problems

Though interpersonal and political problems may be a rarity for the team, it is helpful to determine who will be responsible for intervening should the team encounter such problems. The team may decide that the most appropriate person to assume this role is the team leader. Based on the nature of the problem, however, either another team member or a neutral person who is not officially a team member may be called upon to manage the situation.

Represent the Team to Consumers, Agencies, and the General Public

Team leaders typically are called upon to present the purpose or activities of their teams to school districts, adult service agencies, or other interested groups in the community. Team members may also have opportunities to present to special interest groups the information or products that have resulted from transition team work, such as a manual or videotape that has been developed, or procedures for establishing a new community training program.

Identify and Secure Resources

When teams become immersed in the program implementation process, they often become aware of additional resources that are needed. These unanticipated needs can occur in almost any category of resource, such as staff, equipment, materials and supplies, technical assistance, or inservice training. For a highly motivated team that is eager to see results, this can be a frustrating stumbling block. However, teams that find themselves in this situation may take several courses of action, only one of which is to alter the original plan according to available resources. These options include: (a) Discover creative ways to secure the necessary resources to proceed with the original plan; (b) reexamine the timelines for the problematic objective, task, or activity to determine if postponing the deadline would solve the resource problem; or (c) alter the original plan to fit within available resources.

Discover Creative Ways to Secure the Necessary Resources

This option relies on tapping into resources available in the community, through the school district and adult service agencies, through local philanthropists or service clubs, or through opportunities available at the state or federal levels. For example, equipment, materials and supplies such as paper, video equipment, or telephone use may often be obtained from the school district or adult service agencies that employ team members. Staff time to attend meetings and complete transition team work may also be negotiable with the district or agencies. Inservice training or technical assistance may be available free of charge or with minimal cost through the state department of education or other public agencies such as universities. However, obtaining money to hire a transition team staff person may require the team to seek funds through grant writing or further negotiation with the district or adult service agencies. For example, the team may choose to write a grant in order to hire a work experience coordinator who will develop a secondary special education vocational program.

Reexamine Timelines

In some instances, the solution to lack of resources is simply to alter the timelines for the problematic objective, task, or activity. For example, your team may have undertaken the writing of a transition manual that was to be completed in December. The responsible persons are also serving on another transition team subcommittee for which the tasks (also due in December) must take precedence over the manual. By moving the manual deadline to February, the required personnel time to complete the manual is no longer a problem.

Alter the Original Plan

The third and final alternative to a resource problem is to alter the original plan. When no additional resources are forthcoming, and changing the timeline fails to solve the problem, altering the plan is the final solution. For example, one transition team wrote a grant to fund a large greenhouse that would serve as a worksite for students with disabilities. When the grant did not receive funding, the team changed their plan and developed several small greenhouses built by volunteers with inexpensive materials.

Network with Other Community Transition Teams

Networking provides teams with an opportunity to share materials and ideas. Assuming other community transition teams exist in the region or state, there are several ways for teams to engage in networking, including telephone contact, written communication, and meetings. The frequency and type of networking activities will depend on the needs of the teams and the nature of the work plan. For example, a team that wants to develop or adopt a social skills curriculum could benefit by first determining if any of the other community transition teams have addressed a similar objective. A great deal of time and effort may be saved by obtaining copies of existing materials from other teams or pooling resources to accomplish one objective (e.g., teams work together, with each team taking responsibility for a section of the curriculum).

Meetings of team leaders and/or team members provide another forum for teams to meet and share information in person. At these meetings, teams can present information on transition programs and services. Often the highlights of these meetings are the information sharing and problem-solving sessions, where team leaders and members discuss the problems and the successes they are experiencing in their local communities.

SUMMARY

The program implementation phase is the heart of the community transition team process, as this is when the work of transition teams gets done. Since most of the work is done by volunteers, we suggest developing operational structures and procedures to maximize the efficiency of implementing the team's plan. These procedures include the development of an organizational structure that suits the characteristics of each team's community, the careful specification of roles and responsibilities of the team's leader (or leaders), the identification and securing of resources needed to implement the plan, and facilitation of networking among teams that are working on similar projects.

The implementation of an annual plan can be both exciting and difficult. The excitement derives from attacking major problems that interfere with the provision of good school and transition programs for adolescents with disabilities and their families. The difficulty derives from doing this work with limited resources, including primarily volunteer work. In spite of these difficulties, however, a great deal has been accomplished by transition teams over the years. The next chapter describes how these efforts are evaluated, both to celebrate accomplishments and to lay a foundation for developing a new plan.

CHAPTER 7

Evaluating and Building on Accomplishments

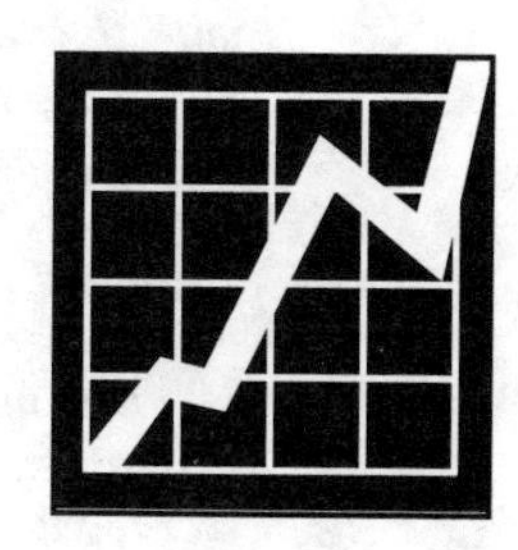

The final phase of the community transition team process is *program evaluation.* Program evaluation includes a systematic review of accomplishments, and a reassessment of needs leading to the development of a new plan.

We encourage community transition teams to evaluate their accomplishments on a yearly basis. Conducting annual evaluations provides an opportunity to take stock of the team's progress to date, celebrate the team's hard work and successes, and plan thoughtfully for the next year. As with earlier phases of the community transition team process, this chapter presents a structured set of procedures that can be used to evaluate the team's accomplishments and plan the activities for next year. As with all other phases of the process, however, the content and focus of the team's evaluation and planning discussions will be completely individualized to reflect its unique circumstances.

Program evaluation is a critical component of the community transition team process because it provides the link between program implementation during a current year and program planning for a subsequent year. Take the time necessary to take full stock of the team's efforts and activities. Improving the capacity of your school(s) and community to better support the transition of youth with disabilities is a continuous journey, and it is easy for teams to fall into the trap of "do, do, and then do some more." This last phase of the community transition team process—evaluation and planning—provides a short respite along the way to remember how far you have come, and to review the roadmap for the next leg of the journey.

The vignette that follows provides an illustration of one team's efforts over several years. It is illustrative of the ways in which a team's activities relate to one another within any given year, and the ways in which activities build cumulatively on one another to create change over time. Two areas of activity are described, both of which address this team's general concern for improving transition services within its community: developing transition planning procedures and increasing family involvement in transition. Read this vignette and think about the implications of building a continuous process of change in your community as your team works together to evaluate and build upon its accomplishments and successes.

VIGNETTE

Developing Transition Planning Procedures

Transition planning for students with disabilities was a priority for many local community teams even before the legislative mandates in the Individuals with Disabilities Education Act ([IDEA] P.L. 101-476) were put into place. This team focused its attention on this area over a 5-year period, beginning with the development of a written transition planning document, *and culminating with ongoing procedures to use specially trained school district personnel to engage in a* transition planning process *with some very difficult students.*

During the first year of effort in this area a small subcommittee of school personnel worked with family members and adult agency representatives to create an individualized transition planning (ITP) form and procedures that would reflect a philosophical emphasis on preparing students for life after high school. Over the course of the school year, this new process was field-tested by a few teachers with a few students. The following year, P.L. 101-476 was passed and transition planning was mandated. Now the school district was convinced of the need to develop transition goals for all students on IEPs. To assist in this process, the community transition team applied for a Cooperative Personnel Planning Grant from the Oregon Department of Education. The grant was used to support inservice training for a group of secondary special education teachers. The training had two components: (1) the new transition services component of IDEA, and (2) the new transition planning documents developed by the team. As a result of this inservice training, the original ITP forms and procedures were modified to meet the requirements of the new legislation. Over the course of the next 2 years, all of the district's certified special education staff (over 200 people) were trained in using the new transition planning forms and procedures.

Now all the special education teachers in the district had a set of written procedures and a form to guide them in their transition planning efforts. However, the transition team felt that more needed to be done to ensure that all students *had the benefit of these procedures. The final step was to apply for another grant to train a group of "transition facilitators" (both teachers and support staff) who would work with students and families to assist them in the planning process. Their mission was to find students who were really struggling with (or who may have dropped out of) the existing school system and to develop a relationship with these students and their families. The facilitators were to help "hook-up" students with needed services and facilitate a process of developing a "person-centered" transition plan.*

Increasing Family Involvement in Transition

During this same timeframe, another subcommittee of the transition team focused its efforts on increasing family involvement in the transition process. This issue was ranked near the top of their formal needs assessment, based on the belief that families needed more information in order to support their students with disabilities during the transition years. With that goal in mind, the team decided to schedule several events to educate family members about the transition process as well as possible transition resources.

During the first year of implementing this plan, the team hosted a Transition Fair. The Fair was arranged in a "Home and Garden Show" format, where various adult service agency representatives set up information tables around the school gym. Parents (and students) could wander around the room, collect materials, and ask questions about possible post-school resources. This Fair was a good way to provide introductory information to a lot of people at the same time. However, some parents wanted more in-depth information and a forum for sharing their concerns. Parent "coffees" were designed to fill that need. The Parent Coffees were evening meetings (complete with pie and coffee) organized around a specific transition topic, such as "Applying for Social Security Benefits" or "Post-Secondary Education Options." At each meeting a guest speaker from the community presented information and school staff were available to answer questions and discuss how these resources might impact specific students.

The coffees were a great success! In fact, the team decided to hold them once a month over the following school year. Yet the team was not totally satisfied. The next step in accomplishing their overall goal of increasing parent involvement in transition was to develop a class for parents of students with disabilities. This class, titled "A Parent's Survival Kit," was developed jointly and team-taught by a high school special education teacher and a local Vocational Rehabilitation counselor who volunteered her time in the evening. The class was revised based on parent input, continues to be offered as an ongoing course at the local community college, and involves staff from several high schools, the community college, and adult service agencies. The class has been a wonderful opportunity for parents to get information and help prepare their students for the transition from school to the community. As one parent commented, "One of the things that helped me through this (transition) process was talking to other parents who have children with disabilities . . . Another was having professionals who could describe the whole picture and offer educated advice."

Note: From "Mobilizing Local Communities To Improve Transition Services," by M. R. Benz, L. Lindstrom, and A. S. Halpern, 1995, *Career Development for Individuals, 18,* pp. 27–29, 31–32. Copyright 1995 by Division on Career Development and Transition. Reprinted with permission.

PROCEDURES FOR EVALUATING AND BUILDING ON THE TEAM'S ACCOMPLISHMENTS

The community transition team evaluation phase involves two components: (a) evaluating the team's activities and accomplishments, and (b) developing an action plan for the next year, using the evaluation information as the foundation for this planning. The team can complete these activities during the last one to two regularly scheduled meetings of the year. However, we encourage you to find a time for a special combination celebration dinner and team meeting. The disadvantage of this latter option is finding a time when all (or almost all) team members can be present, finding a location for a working dinner, and finding funds to have the dinner meeting catered. On the other hand, a dinner meeting provides a special occasion to take stock of the team's progress to date, celebrate the team's hard work and successes, and plan thoughtfully for the next year. Each individual team must decide which option offers the greatest numbers of advantages for team members. Table 7.1 presents a sample agenda for a dinner meeting. This format will be used to describe suggested procedures for completing the evaluation and planning activities that are part of this last phase of the community transition team process.

Evaluating the Team's Accomplishments and Activities

The first part of the evaluation and planning meeting involves two activities: reviewing the team's accomplishments, and reviewing how well the team functioned during the past year. Before beginning this part of the meeting, however, it would be helpful to be sure that all participants know each other. Of course, this will be necessary only if there are new people present at the meeting, which could be the case if any special guests have been invited (e.g., the Director of Special Education or the Coordinator for Secondary Education Services). To ensure that all participants have a common frame of reference, it also is helpful to review the agenda for the meeting and to review the team's action plan. Finally, ask for a volunteer(s) to keep notes of the meeting. These will be helpful for writing a summary report of the team's activities and accomplishments for the year. "Public relations" summaries of this type can be quite helpful in promoting the importance of the team's work. These summaries also can be helpful in the orientation of new team members.

Review Team Accomplishments

No doubt the team has accomplished much, whether it worked on 1 to 2 objectives, or 6 to 8 objectives. In this first part of the meeting, subcommittees and/or team

TABLE 7.1

Sample Agenda for Evaluation and Planning Dinner Meeting

4:00 P.M.	**Introductions (if new members are present)**
4:15 P.M.	**Overview of the Evaluation and Planning Meeting** —Review the agenda. —Review the current action plan. —Identify a person(s) to serve as recorder.
4:30 P.M.	**Evaluation Team Accomplishments and Activities** —Describe and discuss the team's accomplishments (e.g., products and/or programs developed, people trained, additional funds acquired). —Review what worked and what didn't work about the team structure and operational activities (e.g., team process questions).
5:30 P.M.	**Break for Dinner**
6:00 P.M.	**Development of the Action Plan for Next Year** —Identify new or "carry-over" goals and objectives. —Develop tasks and timelines for each objective. —Reconvene as a group and review all objectives.
7:30 P.M.	**Establishment of Team Structure for Next Year** —Identify persons and resources for each objective. —Establish subcommittees and operational procedures. —Identify person(s) to write a summary of team accomplishments. —Set a time and place for the next meeting.
8:00 P.M.	**Adjourn Meeting**

members have the opportunity to describe what they have accomplished. If the team accomplished its work via subcommittees and met as an entire team regularly throughout the year, then most team members will already be somewhat aware of the activities and accomplishments of the subcommittees. Nevertheless, this is a time to highlight and celebrate the work of the team. If products have been developed (e.g., a transition manual, a social skills curriculum), or if there are other outcomes from the subcommittee's work (e.g., materials and evaluation results from a staff inservice training), this is a great time to share these results of the team's work. As part of this presentation, ask subcommittees to identify additional resources they acquired to complete their work (e.g., additional direct funding, in-kind support).

Review Team Activities

In addition to reviewing the team's accomplishments, it is important to take stock of how well the team functioned in the past year. Table 7.2 provides 10 questions to help structure this discussion. These 10 questions are organized under two general categories: team membership and team operations. There are several ways these questions can be used to facilitate a discussion of how well the team functioned in the past year.

We suggest team members (and others, if you choose) review these questions prior to the evaluation and planning meeting. Team members' review of these questions can range from informal (e.g., ask them to read and think about the ques-

TABLE 7.2
Sample Team Process Questions To Guide Discussion of Team Functioning

Team Membership

1. Is the team able to recruit and orient new members successfully?
2. Does the team include a balanced representation of school personnel, community members, and consumers?
3. Has team membership been maintained at a stable level or has it increased?
4. Do team members participate consistently in team activities?
5. Do team members understand their roles and responsibilities?

Team Operations

6. Does the team meet on a regular basis?
7. Are team meetings well organized and productive?
8. Are subcommittees able to complete their work in an effective and timely manner?
9. Does the team have the support of key administrative personnel?
10. Is the team able to collaborate as needed with other related school and/or community initiatives?

tions prior to the meeting) to formal (e.g., create a scale and ask members to rate each item and write comments to support their ratings).

Regardless of which approach is adopted, discuss both "what worked" and "what didn't work" with regard to how well the team has functioned in the past year. If the team has gotten to this point in the community transition team process, obviously, it has done some things quite well in terms of its functioning. Yet, few teams function so well that there is nothing to improve. Keeping both of these perspectives in mind will help the team continually "fine tune" its operations in subsequent years.

If the team is completing its evaluation and planning activities in a special dinner meeting, now is a good time to break for dinner. If the team is completing these activities through two separate meetings, set a date, time, and location for the next meeting.

Develop an Action Plan for the Next Year

At this point in the meeting, the team is ready to use the evaluation information it discussed on accomplishments and activities to develop an action plan for the next year. Complete the following two activities in order to develop the basic framework for the next year's plan: (a) identify new or "carry-over" goals and objectives, and (b) develop tasks and timelines for each selected objective.

Identify New or Carry-Over Goals and Objectives

There are several options for identifying the goals and objectives that will become the focus of program improvement efforts for the next year. You might want to consider carrying over one or more goals and/or objectives from the current year. Remember that each of the current objectives was chosen originally as *one way* of addressing a high priority program improvement goal. As the team now takes stock of its progress, it is possible that one or more of the objectives in the plan will not be completed. It is also possible that the current objectives being addressed only partially achieve the goals that were identified as high priority during the previous needs assessment activity. If the team chooses to work further on an existing goal, return to the list of objectives created during the initial needs assessment activities for ideas on how to further address an existing goal. As a starting point, ask the following two questions:

1. Will the team continue to work on any objectives that are specified in the current plan but are not yet finished?
2. Will the team decide to work on any new objectives for any goals that are contained in the current plan?

The team is now ready to complete laying the foundation for the next annual plan. If the team decides that it wants to do more work next year in addition to completing any unfinished objectives or addressing new objectives for existing goals, then it must next identify which *new* goals and objectives it wants to designate for attention. In order to reach this decision, review the team's top-priority goals and associated objectives as identified in the initial needs assessment.

At some point, the team will decide that it must conduct another needs assessment to determine top-priority program improvement goals and objectives. This may occur because: (a) the team has completed work on the existing goals to its satisfaction, (b) the composition and membership of the team has changed such that the original needs assessment is no longer valid, or (c) changes have occurred in the school(s) or community such that a new direction for the team's improvement activities is warranted. If team members feel a new needs assessment is required in order to develop the next year's plan, follow the guidelines provided in the needs assessment chapter and incorporate this new information into planning activities. When final decisions about new goals and associated objectives have been made, the team is ready to develop tasks and timelines for each selected objective.

Develop Tasks and Timelines for Each Objective

Once a set of objectives has been identified, team members must develop tasks and timelines for each selected objective. Depending upon the number of team members present at the evaluation and planning meeting, and the number of selected objectives, the team may either develop tasks and timelines in subgroups or as an entire team. The general rule here is to use an approach that will complete this step as efficiently as possible *and* will maximize the participation of all team members. It is important to "demystify" the task analysis concept and to help all team members feel that they can create a set of logical steps to go from point A to point B.

Once tasks and timelines have been created for each objective, team members should review the proposed task analysis for each objective in order to determine whether or not the sequence of tasks is a good work plan for the team. Engage team members in a discussion of the task analysis "as a whole." Is there a logical starting point for the objective? Does the sequence of tasks make sense or are there critical steps missing in the identified sequence? Does the identified set of tasks allow the team to achieve the outcome intended for this objective? Make revisions to the task analysis and timeline for each objective based on the outcomes of this discussion. Review the final task analysis for each objective with the entire team to obtain consensus on the work scope.

Reconvene as a Group (If Necessary) and Review All Objectives

When the team has completed the designation of tasks and timelines for all objectives specified in the preliminary plan, take a moment to consider the cumulative impact of the decisions. Have too many tasks been scheduled to be completed during any given month? If so, make some modifications in the timelines. Is the total schedule overly ambitious and not likely to succeed? If so, consider eliminating some tasks, or perhaps even an entire standard and objective combination. Remember, during the initial program planning efforts, a follow-up meeting was scheduled to allow the team to look at the tasks by a timeline calendar of events in order to help with these decisions. To conserve time, this extra meeting has been eliminated during the replanning stage of the community transition team process. If this extra step is needed, however, feel free to modify these suggested procedures to allow for a calendar to be produced before making final decisions about commitments.

Establish Team Structure for the Next Year

The meeting is now nearing an end. In this last part, the team will be putting the finishing touches on its action plan and establishing procedures to guide the program improvement efforts during the next year.

Identify Persons and Resources for Each Objective

Team members should identify the resources needed, the subcommittee chair(s), and the other people who need to be involved in the implementation of each standard and objective combination in the plan. In some cases, decisions at this point may be only to *seek* additional resources that are needed to do a good job on a particular task. These additional resources can be money, "in-kind" contributions, and/or personnel time. Some teams use this opportunity to identify new potential members who might be recruited to do one or more specific tasks in the plan.

Establish Subcommittees and Operational Procedures

Lastly, discuss how the team will function during its next year of operation. Taking into consideration the results of the earlier discussion on how well the team functioned during the past year, and the decisions made regarding the focus of efforts in the next year, review and determine (a) your team's meeting procedures (e.g., frequency and location), (b) the role of the team leader (or co-leaders), and (c) the role and functioning of subcommittees.

Wrap Up the Meeting

You are at the finish line. As final activities, identify a person or small group of persons who will be responsible for translating the team's decisions into an action plan for the next year. Also, identify a person or small group of persons who will be responsible for gathering the actual products that emerged from the past year of activities and for summarizing the results of the meeting into a concise report. Together, the team's products and the meeting report will provide a great tool for sharing the team's work with prospective new members, key administrators, and other stakeholders who are concerned with transition services and outcomes for youth with disabilities.

SUMMARY

With the completion of the activities described in this chapter, your transition team will have come full circle in the implementation of the community transition team process. The progress of the past year will be documented, and the team will know what remains to be done to improve services in your community. The team will also have a set of precise guidelines for continuing its work, as specified in its new annual plan.

In closing, briefly recall the basic rationale for doing all of this work. As we move into the next century, there appears to be a strong commitment—at local, state, and federal levels—to improve secondary special education and transition programs for adolescents and young adults with disabilities. In order to take advantage of these opportunities, it is necessary to improve our *capacity* to deliver good services in our local communities, whether these communities be urban or rural, highly developed or struggling, rich or poor. A system is needed to help each community improve its offering of programs and services, regardless of the starting point from which any given community begins. The transition team is a fundamental part of such a system, and the members of the team are the heart of this effort. We hope that the procedures we have suggested will provide a useful set of tools for engaging in productive efforts to improve secondary special education and transition programs for students with disabilities and their families.

APPENDIX A
Sample District Strategic Planning Tool

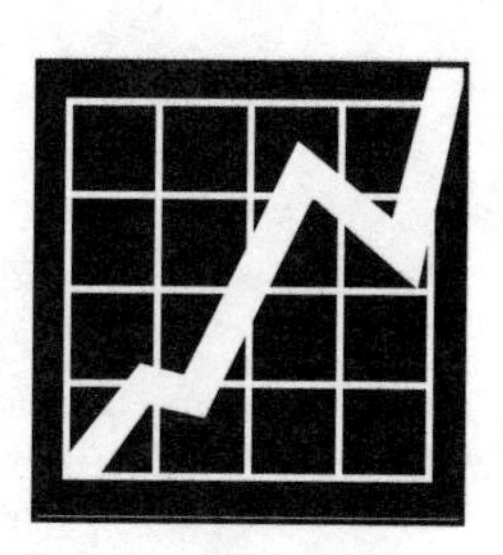

OVERVIEW

The Educational Plan for Student Success (EPSS) is a comprehensive, long-range planning, implementation, and evaluation tool designed to lead to improved student learning and school improvement. The plan is student centered, system-wide, and cuts across all disciplines and programs. It includes clear expectations, implementation strategies, and an evaluation component. The EPSS is developed and implemented after the first on-site Standards for Excellence Accreditation visit. Evaluation of the plan in terms of student progress is part of the ongoing accreditation process. Further development and refinement of the EPSS is a continuous process.

EPSS Process: The First 6 Years

Year	Activities
Year 1	Develop self-study.
Year 2	Verify self-study through the State Department of Education (SDE) on-site accreditation visit. Develop EPSS.
Year 3	Develop EPSS. Submit EPSS to SDE for review (one calendar year after accreditation visit). Implement EPSS. Develop baseline student progress data.
Year 4	Implement EPSS. Assess and evaluate EPSS. Assess and evaluate student progress.
Year 5	Implement EPSS. Verify EPSS through SDE on-site accreditation visit. Assess and evaluate EPSS. Assess and evaluate student progress.
Year 6	Implement EPSS. Assess and evaluate EPSS. Assess and evaluate student progress (summative). Modify and revise plan as needed. Submit revisions to SDE for review.
EPSS Cycle: Years 7 Through 12 and Subsequent Years	
Year 7	Implement modified EPSS. Assess and evaluate EPSS. Assess and evaluate student progress.
Year 8	Implement EPSS. Assess and evaluate EPSS. Assess and evaluate student progress (summative). Verify EPSS and student progress through SDE on-site accreditation visit.
Year 9	Implement EPSS. Revisit self-study, EPSS, assessment, and evaluation information. Modify and/or develop EPSS, as needed.

Note: Adapted from *Educational Plan for Student Success,* by the New Mexico State Department of Education, 1996, Santa Fe: Author.

Year 10	Implement EPSS. Assess and evaluate EPSS. Assess and evaluate student progress.
Year 11	Implement EPSS. Assess and evaluate EPSS. Assess and evaluate student progress (summative).
Year 12	Implement EPSS. Revisit self-study, EPSS, assessment, and evaluation information. Modify and/or develop EPSS, as needed.
Subsequent years	Repeat sequence of activities for years 7 through 12.

GETTING STARTED

The first step in developing an effective EPSS is to identify the EPSS planning team. While the entire school community is involved in all stages of the EPSS process, the EPSS planning team develops the actual plan and oversees its implementation and evaluation. This team is representative of the diversity of the community and includes representation of all the district's partners in education (i.e., students, parents, community members, social service providers, institutions of higher education, etc.). Effective planning teams usually consist of no more than 25 members. Once the planning team is identified, the school community begins developing the EPSS. The assigned State Department of Education (SDE) EPSS/Accreditation Team Leader for the district or school is available for technical assistance throughout all stages of the EPSS process.

PREPARING TO DEVELOP THE EPSS

The aim of the EPSS is to improve student learning and success. The student-centered process requires that the diverse needs of all students be identified and addressed, utilizing the resources within the school community. An effective EPSS identifies and aligns quality programs and services, and integrates all elements of the educational process into a comprehensive plan. How is this accomplished? Critical to the process is the identification of student needs. Information about the student population, performance, demographics, and so forth, is generated through the accreditation self-study. This information serves as a starting point for identifying student needs and developing baseline information. Other information to build from includes the accreditation report; district or school (accreditation) focus areas; interviews of school staff, students, and parents; and information generated through community meetings. Once needs have been identified, an in-depth assessment of the school community's resources takes place. The entire spectrum of resources—local, state, and federal—is examined in light of how resources can best be utilized to improve student learning and success.

DEVELOPING THE EPSS

Once needs and resources are assessed, the EPSS is developed. Many strategic, long-range planning models and processes exist, including North Central Association (NCA), Cambridge, Learning's Shades of Change, Total Quality Management, and others. The State Department of Education does not mandate that a particular model be utilized; however, it has set minimum expectations for the development of the EPSS: (a) The broad school community must be involved in all steps of the process; (b) the plan and the goals/focus areas must be student centered; and

(c) the goals/focus areas and objectives must be measurable so that student progress can be documented. Regardless of the model used, districts and schools are expected to address the following questions: Where are we now? Where do we need to be? How will we get there? How will we know we are making progress toward our goals?

WHAT HAPPENS AFTER THE PLAN IS DEVELOPED?

Once the EPSS is written, it must be approved by the local board of education. Upon board approval, it is submitted to the SDE for review. If necessary, revisions are made, and additional or supplemental information is provided. A formal written agreement is established between the district or school and SDE regarding expectations for the plan and its implementation. Once the plan is reviewed by the district or school and approved by the SDE, it is implemented. The district or school, through the EPSS planning team, evaluates the effectiveness of the plan on an ongoing basis and reports progress to its school community.

WHAT ABOUT ACCOUNTABILITY?

Accountability is an expectation at both the local and state levels. The district or school is continually accountable to its school community. It conducts ongoing reviews of progress in meeting the goals of the plan and reports student progress to the school community. In designing this accountability process, the district or school must use evaluation measures that are understandable to the public. Other accountability measures include the following: At the annual SDE program and budget review, the district or school must demonstrate that its budget reflects the goals and objectives of the EPSS; it demonstrates progress toward meeting the goals and objectives of the EPSS during the SDE on-site accreditation reviews.

DISTRICT SELF-STUDY MODEL

PART I: UNIQUE DISTRICT INSIGHTS AND ANALYSES

Directions

The district will synthesize and analyze information and input from all district schools and stakeholders, including administrators, teachers, parents, students, business partners, and other community members.

Required Components

1. Current objectives
2. Description of district student population
3. Community insights
4. Quality of Education survey results
5. Other district identified data

PART II: DISTRICT DATA TREND ANALYSIS

Directions

The district will review and verify the analysis of each school site's *Indicators of Student Success.* All information will then be synthesized and analyzed in order to determine the district status.

Required Components

1. Have all schools in the district gathered and analyzed information mandated through state-wide testing?
2. Have all schools in the district gathered and analyzed information needed for the Accountability Report?
3. Have all schools in the district gathered and analyzed self-study assessment data?
4. Have all schools in the district gathered supporting assessment data?

PART III: REVIEW AND ANALYSIS OF CURRENT MANAGEMENT ORGANIZATION

Directions

The district will gather and analyze information on programs provided by the district.

Required Components

1. Current status of curriculum in all required programs and courses
2. Current status of all federal programs
3. Current status of community involvement
4. Current status of how the budget is supporting programs in relation to student needs

5. Current status of school and central office communication
6. Current status of Evaluation Plan for Licensed Personnel
7. Current status of staff development

PART IV: DISTRICT COMPLIANCE REVIEW

Directions

The district will review the list of areas of compliance in the Accreditation Manual and determine compliance responsibility: school site or district or both. The district should then review its status in terms of the compliance areas. Finally, the district should analyze its strengths and needs in relation to these identified compliance areas.

PART V: DISTRICT CULMINATING ANALYSIS IN RELATION TO STANDARDS FOR EXCELLENCE: IDENTIFICATION OF GOALS/FOCUS AREAS

A. Current District Status in Relation to the *Standards for Excellence*

Utilizing data and preliminary analysis from Parts I through IV, the district will determine its current status in relation to the *Standards for Excellence.* The *Standards for Excellence* is a guiding document for determining focus areas or goals. The culminating analysis should provide a comprehensive picture of the district and should be the vehicle for drawing conclusions as to strengths, needs, and unanswered questions that impact student success.

B. Future District Direction in Relation to the *Standards for Excellence*

Goals/focus areas are derived from the analysis and synthesis of all self-study information that impacts student success. Goals/focus areas should be stated in terms of improved student learning and/or district improvement.

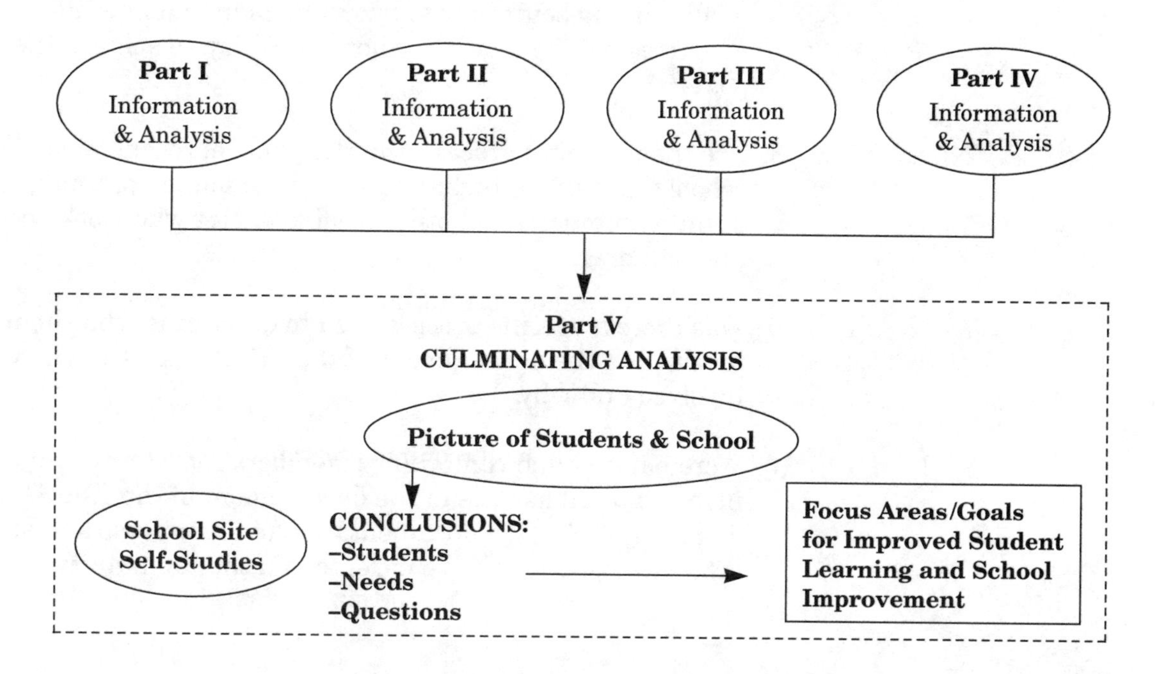

EPSS REVIEW CHECKLIST

This checklist should be used as a tool to assist the district in the development of the EPSS in order to ensure that the EPSS process and plan include the required components. During the EPSS review and approval process, the checklist will be used to determine if the district's EPSS meets the required criteria.

Y N NI	***Directions:*** *Circle the appropriate letters before each question.* ***Y = YES N = NO NI = NEEDS IMPROVEMENT*** *Provide supporting information for each response.*

GENERAL

Y N NI 1. Is the EPSS tied to the self-study and mission? In what way?

Y N NI 2. Is the EPSS a strategic plan to improve student learning and success?

Y N NI 3. Is the EPSS system-wide and across curricula?

Y N NI 4. Is the EPSS more comprehensive than the identified focus areas? Describe how it goes beyond the focus areas.

Y N NI 5. How does the EPSS relate to the last accreditation report in terms of strengths, concerns, and areas of noncompliance?

Y N NI 6. Does the EPSS incorporate all educational and community resources available and needed to support student learning and success?

Y N NI 7. Does the EPSS specify how the budget will coordinate the use of all funding sources to support the plan and how additional resources will be secured, when necessary, to achieve the goals?

Y N NI 8. Are the planning process and the plan representative of the school community, including school personnel, parents, community members, and other local agencies who work with area children?

Y N NI 9. Was there a specific process used to determine who should be involved in the development of the EPSS? Explain who was involved and why.

Y N NI 10. Were parents and community members represented and involved in all aspects of the development of the EPSS? In what ways? Provide documentation of the process and specific activities used to involve parents and the community.

Y N NI 11. Were efforts made to contact and involve all parents, including those who do not typically participate in school-related activities, in all aspects of the EPSS process? Describe these efforts.

Y N NI 12. Are all components of the plan clearly stated?

STEP 1: WHERE ARE WE NOW?

SELF-STUDY: IDENTIFICATION OF STUDENT NEEDS

Y N NI 1. Does the self-study process use a variety of methods for gathering information? Were these methods appropriate and adequate?

Y N NI 2. Does the self-study process identify the needs of all students?

Y N NI 3. Are the special needs of particular populations of students identified through the self-study process?

Y N NI 4. Does the EPSS use appropriate student data to determine student learning and success and identify student needs?

Y N NI 5. Does the self-study process identify available and needed community resources to support identified student needs?

STEP 2: WHERE DO WE NEED TO BE?

GOALS/FOCUS AREAS

Y N NI 1. Is the self-study information analyzed in light of the *Standards for Excellence* and the Competency Frameworks, and were they used to develop goals/focus areas?

Y N NI 2. Are the goals/focus areas specifically tied to the needs of all students identified through the self-study process?

Y N NI 3. Are the goals/focus areas statements of what all students will know and be able to do within the context of *Standards for Excellence* and the Competency Frameworks?

Y N NI 4. Are specific measures that will indicate student progress identified?

Y N NI 5. Do the goals/focus areas also address school improvement and existing successful efforts?

STEP 3: HOW WILL WE GET THERE?

ACTION PLANS

Y N NI 1. Are the action plans district-wide rather than site specific?

Y N NI 2. Is each objective measurable and tied to the goals/focus areas?

Y N NI 3. Do all implementation strategies lead to the attainment of stated objectives?

Y N NI 4. Are there timelines for implementation and evaluation of action plans?

Y N NI 5. Do the action plans indicate the persons responsible for tasks?

Y N NI 6. Are the action plans realistic in terms of available resources and timeframes?

STEP 4: HOW WILL WE KNOW WE ARE MAKING PROGRESS TOWARD OUR GOALS?

ONGOING AND COMPREHENSIVE ASSESSMENT AND EVALUATION

Y N NI 1. Is evaluation clearly tied to the goals/focus areas?

Y N NI 2. Do the evaluation components clearly indicate the level of student progress?

Y N NI 3. Are the evaluation components appropriate for students, school, and district?

Y N NI 4. Can the evaluation results be easily communicated to the school community?

APPENDIX B

Sample Interagency Agreement

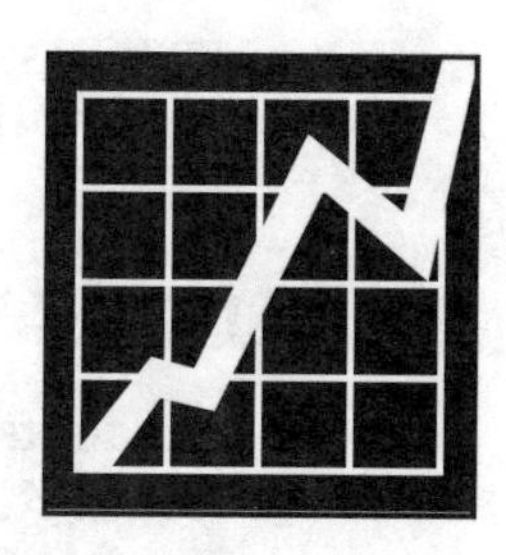

I. PURPOSE

The purpose of this agreement is to facilitate the integration and coordination of services to eligible secondary students. The intent is to integrate the activities of education and rehabilitation services to provide a continuum of services which will meet the needs of all students with disabilities. The integrated continuum of services will

A. Assure that all students with disabilities as defined by the Individuals with Disabilities Education Act (IDEA), the Rehabilitation Act of 1973, as amended, and the Americans with Disabilities Act, receive appropriate and necessary services;

B. Coordinate services to students with disabilities so as to maximize learner outcomes and provide for a successful transition to appropriate employment and independent living;

C. Formalize referral procedures to appropriate agency(s) to ensure students with disabilities are provided opportunities for services;

D. Ensure joint planning of Individual Education Plans (IEPs), Individual Transition Plans (ITPs), Individual Service Plans (ISPs), and Individual Written Rehabilitation Plans (IWRPs) for each student with disabilities eligible for Division of Vocational Rehabilitation, Developmental Disabilities Division, Mental Health Division, or Social Security Administration services within the member school districts of the Region IX Education Cooperative;

E. Ensure coordination of service delivery and follow-up/along with education/social/rehabilitation services continuum as identified in an IEP which includes an ITP and ISP and IWRP if needed, as in D. above; and

F. Ensure joint training between cooperating agencies for staff development and other activities.

II. GOAL

This agreement will provide for the unified delivery of integrated transition planning services to Region IX Education Cooperative (REC IX) special education students, ages 16 to 21. The intent is to create an integrated service system flexible enough to meet the needs of all special education students **within the available**

Note. From "Memorandum of Understanding Among the Developmental Disabilities Division, the Mental Health Division, the Division of Vocational Rehabilitation, the Department of Labor, the Social Security Administration, Area Community Colleges, and the School Districts in the Region IX Education Cooperative," by the Region IX Education Cooperative, 1997, Ruidoso, New Mexico: Author.

resources. The focus is on maximizing opportunities for students while eliminating limitations and obstacles.

III. ELIGIBILITY

Students with disabilities 16 to 21 years old may be eligible for Division of Vocational Rehabilitation (DVR), Developmental Disabilities Division (DDD), Mental Health Division (MHD) through The Counseling Center, Department of Labor (DOL)/Job Training Partnership Act (JTPA), and the United States Social Security Administration (SSA) services under this memorandum of understanding if they meet the following requirements:

A. The student has a currently approved IEP which includes an ITP in place, and/or

B. The student has a disabling condition which constitutes a substantial vocational handicap and/or a barrier to employment.

IV. FUNCTIONS AND RESPONSIBILITIES

The Division of Vocational Rehabilitation (DVR), the Developmental Disabilities Division (DDD) and the Mental Health Division (MHD) of the Department of Health through the Counseling Center, the Department of Labor (DOL/JTPA), the Social Security Administration (SSA), Eastern New Mexico University–Roswell, Eastern New Mexico University–Ruidoso Instruction Center, New Mexico State University–Alamogordo, the Region IX Education Cooperative, and the Capitan, Carrizozo, Cloudcroft, Corona, Hondo Valley, Ruidoso and Tularosa School Districts agree to cooperate in providing appropriate transition services to students with physical and/or mental disabilities, in order to assure the student's entry into suitable employment and independent living. It is mutually agreed that the following steps and procedures will be utilized to accomplish this goal.

1. At the beginning of each school year, all parties to this Memorandum of Understanding will meet with appropriate school personnel, i.e., counselors, diagnosticians/department heads, principals and the REC IX Transition Coordinator, to provide an overview of the comprehensive transition services available, including eligibility requirements and services offered.

2. Following the meeting with the participating agencies, special education teachers will identify students, beginning at age 16, with physical and/or learning disabilities for referral to the DVR/DDD/MHD/DOL/JTPA/SSA or other service providers if appropriate. A release of information will be secured by the school prior to the referral the student to DVR/DDD/MHD/DOL/SSA. A list of prospective clients will be forwarded to the DVR and DOL/JTPA counselors in Alamogordo, the DDD Office in Las Cruces, and the SSA Offices in Las Cruces and Roswell by October 15th annually. The DVR/DDD/MHD/DOL/JTPA/SSA personnel will meet the student, school representative and REC IX Transition Coordinator to review and determine if an application for services is appropriate.

3. The DVR Counselors, DDD staff, MHD staff, DOL/JTPA staff, SSA staff, ENMU–Roswell, ENMU–Ruidoso, and NMSU–Alamogordo staff will provide consultative services in the area of vocational and career planning and job engineering to school counselors, diagnosticians and/or department heads,

and other appropriate staff, for potential vocational rehabilitation students, to assist in the development of the IEP/IWRP/ISP during the two year period prior to the student's projected school program completion.

4. During the student's senior or last year in school, the DVR counselor will accept and process the student's application for vocational rehabilitation services. The student and appropriate education personnel will be notified of the eligibility decision. The DVR counselor will develop the IWRP or make a vocational recommendation for each eligible student.

5. DVR will provide eligible students, as resources allow, vocational rehabilitation services directly related to achieving the planned employment outcome. These services must be specified in the IWRP.

6. Interagency training will take place annually between DVR, DDD, MHD, DOL/JTPA, SSA, ENMU–Roswell, ENMU–Ruidoso Instruction Center, NMSU–Alamogordo, the LEAs and REC IX. REC IX will coordinate this training among the identified agencies.

7. Annually, all parties of this Memorandum of Understanding will meet with selected personnel from each school district and the REC IX Transition Coordinator to determine the effectiveness of this agreement and to effect changes as needed. This annual review will be conducted in the Spring of each year, to be held no later than April 30th. Those persons/agency representatives who attend this annual meeting will sign a one page agreement to continue the Memorandum of Understanding as written or will make written recommendations to update/make changes to the Memorandum of Understanding. These recommendations will be incorporated into the current Memorandum of Understanding and forwarded for approval to those agencies who signed the original Memorandum of Understanding.

LOCAL EDUCATIONAL AGENCIES (LEAs) WILL . . .*

1. Acknowledge its/their role in providing transition services for students with disabilities and/or with an active IEP;

2. (subsequent statements will vary by agency)

REGION IX EDUCATION COOPERATIVE WILL . . .*

THE STATEWIDE PARENT ORGANIZATION WILL . . .*

THE DIVISION OF VOCATIONAL REHABILITATION WILL . . .*

V. REFERRAL PROCEDURES

The REC IX School Districts will be the lead agency(s) in the referral process. Listed below are the steps to be taken by the REC IX School Districts to refer students to agencies providing support and/or funding for students with disabilities. It is the intent of all of the organizations to share information/records to the greatest extent allowed by law. No information will be shared between agencies without a signed release by the parent/student. An original of each signed release by the parent/student shall be retained by the agency that information is released to.

**Note.* The complete document may be viewed in the Appendixes of the *Adult Agencies: Linkages for Adolescents in Transition* book (Cozzens, Dowdy, & Smith, 1999) in the PRO-ED Series on Transition.

The Division of Vocational Rehabilitation

Not later than October 15th of each school year, the REC IX School Districts will provide the DVR Counselors with an appropriate list of students in each school district who may qualify for DVR support. This list will include School, student's name, student's grade, age, Student I.D. number, and student's disability, approved by a student who is of age or with written parental consent. Additionally, during the year prior to exit, the REC IX School Districts will provide DVR a consolidated list of projected exiting students (juniors) for the next school year.

Developmental Disability Division

Not later than October 15th of each school year, the REC IX School Districts will provide the Developmental Disability Division with an appropriate list of senior/exiting students with Developmental Disabilities. This list will include school, student's name, address and telephone number, and the Student I.D. number, disability, approved by a student who is of age or with written parental consent. Additionally, during the Spring semester, the REC IX School Districts will provide DDD a consolidated list of projected exiting students (juniors) for the next school year.

The Counseling Center, Representing The Mental Health Division

Not later than October 15th of each school year, the REC IX School Districts will provide the Mental Health Division with an appropriate list of senior/exiting students with disabilities. This list will include school, student's name, address and telephone number, and the Student I.D. number, disability, approved by a student who is of age or with written parental consent. Additionally, during the Spring semester, the REC IX School Districts will provide Mental Health Division a consolidated list of projected exiting students (juniors) for the next school year.

The New Mexico Department of Labor

Not later than February, the REC IX School Districts will provide the New Mexico Department of Labor with an appropriate list of graduating/exiting seniors with disabilities. This list will include the student's name, high school, grade, I.D. Number, address, telephone number, a copy of a photo identification and disability approved by the parent and/or the student who is of age.

The Social Security Administration

The REC IX School Districts will refer students to the Social Security Administration on a case by case basis. To refer, the student/family will call 800-772-1213 and tell the SSA that they desire to apply for SSI/SSDI. The SSA will then begin the screen process to ensure that the student qualifies for support. Upon referral, the student/school district shall provide all pertinent records allowed by law.

Eastern New Mexico University–Roswell

The REC IX School Districts will refer students to the Eastern New Mexico–Roswell on a case by case basis, but will provide Eastern New Mexico–Roswell a list of potential students not later than October 15th during each school year. The School

District will contact the Eastern New Mexico–Roswell when a student is identified who desires to attend the Eastern New Mexico–Roswell or who might benefit from their classes.

Eastern New Mexico University Instructional Center–Ruidoso

The REC IX School Districts will refer students to the Eastern New Mexico University Instructional Center–Ruidoso on a case by case basis, but will provide Eastern New Mexico University Instructional Center–Ruidoso a list of potential students not later than October 15th during each school year. The School District will contact the Eastern New Mexico University Instructional Center–Ruidoso when a student is identified who desires to attend the Eastern New Mexico University Instructional Center–Ruidoso or who might benefit from their classes.

New Mexico State University–Alamogordo

The REC IX School Districts will refer students to the New Mexico State University–Alamogordo on a case by case basis, but will provide New Mexico State University–Alamogordo a list of potential students not later than October 15th during each school year. The School District will contact the New Mexico State University–Alamogordo when a student is identified who desires to attend the New Mexico State University–Alamogordo or who might benefit from their classes.

VI. EFFECTIVE DATE AND TERMINATION

This MOU shall take effect when signed by all parties, and shall remain in effect until terminated. Any party may terminate its participation in this MOU by providing ninety days advance notice in writing to the other party.

IN WITNESS WHEREOF, the following signatures are affixed:

Developmental Disabilities Division

by: ______________________________ ______________
Division Director Date

Division of Vocational Rehabilitation

by: ______________________________ ______________
DVR Director Date

Region IX Education Cooperative

by: ______________________________ ______________
Executive Director Date

Mental Health Division

by: ______________________________ ____________
Director, The Counseling Center Date

Social Security Administration

by: ______________________________ ____________
District Manager, Roswell Date

by: ______________________________ ____________
Branch Manager, Las Cruces Date

Department of Labor

by: ______________________________ ____________
New Mexico Department of Labor, Area Director Date

Eastern New Mexico University–Roswell

by: ______________________________ ____________
Provost Date

Eastern New Mexico University Instruction Center–Ruidoso

by: ______________________________ ____________
Center Director Date

New Mexico State University–Alamogordo

by: ______________________________ ____________
Provost Date

Developmental Disabilities Division, Mental Health Division, New Mexico Department Of Labor, Division Of Vocational Rehabilitation, Eastern New Mexico University–Roswell, Eastern New Mexico University–Ruidoso Instruction Center, New Mexico State University–Alamogordo, The School Districts Of Region IX Education Cooperative, And The Social Security Administration Joint Authorization For Release Of Information

I, ____ SSN: __________________

Date of Birth: __________________ Date of Authorization: ____________________

Hereby request/authorize ____

to release the information specified below to me or, if preferred to:

_____ Developmental Disabilities Division
_____ _______________ School District
_____ Social Security Administration
_____ ENMU–Roswell
_____ The Counseling Center
_____ Division of Vocational Rehabilitation
_____ The NM Department of Labor
_____ NMSU–Alamogordo
_____ ENMU–Ruidoso Instruction Center
_____ Other

The information to be disclosed is:

_____ Medical Records
_____ Dental Records
_____ Psychological/Psychiatric Records
_____ Diagnostic Records
_____ High School Transcripts
_____ University/College Transcripts
_____ Work Study Information
_____ Other ____________________

I authorize that a photo copy of this authorization be accepted with the same authority as the original. This information will be treated as confidential and is to be used only for the purposes of determining eligibility for services by the Developmental Disabilities Division, the Mental Health Division, the Division of Vocational Rehabilitation, the New Mexico Department of Labor, Eastern New Mexico–Roswell, Eastern New Mexico University–Ruidoso Instruction Center, New Mexico State University–Alamogordo, and the Social Security Administration. Any agency receiving this information is directed to treat it as confidential in accordance with the Family Education Rights and Privacy Act (34 CFR 99).

This authorization dated _______________ is good only for 30 days or earlier if revoked by me in writing at which time it will expire and no further release of records shall be made under its terms. Furthermore, I understand that I can revoke this authorization at any time, except with respect to action already taken by the above noted parties in reliance upon it. I also understand that I have a right to examine and copy the information to be disclosed and to submit clarifying or correcting statements and other documentation of reasonable length for inclusion with confidential information. Denial of access to such records is granted only when a physician or other mental health or professional believes and notes in my records that such disclosure would not be in my best interest.

I certify that this form has been explained to me. I have read the contents of this form or the contents have been read to me. I understand its contents. The explanation of the contents was made and all blanks or statements requiring insertion or completion were filled in and all shall be honored by those to whom it is sent or provided.

Signature of Client	Date
Address	Phone
Signature of Parent or Guardian	Date
Witnessed By	Date

APPENDIX C

Sample Program Standards Instrument

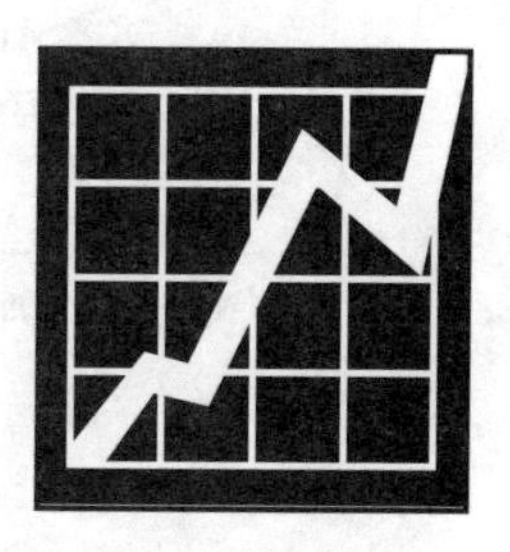

COMMUNITY TRANSITION TEAM MODEL: NEEDS ASSESSMENT INSTRUMENT

For each standard listed below, circle your rating of the importance for the standard (value), and the extent to which programs in your community are meeting the standard (current status). Please complete the value scale for *all* items. The current status scale should be completed *only* if you are familiar with the content being described. As in the following example, circle one number only for each scale.

Transition team members have the mild manners of Clark Kent, the endurance of King Kong, and the humor of Phyllis Diller.

Value				Current Status			
Critical	Important	Somewhat Useful	Not Important	Completely Achieved	Mostly Achieved	Partially Achieved	Not Achieved
(3)	2	1	0	0	1	(2)	3

CURRICULUM AND INSTRUCTION

1. Students with disabilities receive appropriate remedial academic instruction, which prepares them for functioning in their community, including the possibility of postsecondary education.

Value				Current Status			
Critical	Important	Somewhat Useful	Not Important	Completely Achieved	Mostly Achieved	Partially Achieved	Not Achieved
3	2	1	0	0	1	2	3

2. Students with disabilities receive appropriate vocational instruction, which prepares them for jobs in their community.

Value				Current Status			
Critical	Important	Somewhat Useful	Not Important	Completely Achieved	Mostly Achieved	Partially Achieved	Not Achieved
3	2	1	0	0	1	2	3

Note: From *Community Transition Team Model: Needs Assessment Instrument,* by A. S. Halpern, L. E. Lindstrom, M. R. Benz, and R. S. Rothstrom, 1991, Eugene, OR: University of Oregon Press. Reprinted with permission.

3. Students with disabilities receive appropriate instruction in independent living, which prepares them for functioning as young adults in their community.

Value				Current Status			
Critical	Important	Somewhat Useful	Not Important	Completely Achieved	Mostly Achieved	Partially Achieved	Not Achieved
3	2	1	0	0	1	2	3

4. Students with disabilities receive appropriate instruction in social and interpersonal skills, which prepares them for interacting effectively with people in their community.

Value				Current Status			
Critical	Important	Somewhat Useful	Not Important	Completely Achieved	Mostly Achieved	Partially Achieved	Not Achieved
3	2	1	0	0	1	2	3

5. Students with disabilities receive appropriate instruction in leisure and recreation skills, which prepares them for leisure opportunities within their community.

Value				Current Status			
Critical	Important	Somewhat Useful	Not Important	Completely Achieved	Mostly Achieved	Partially Achieved	Not Achieved
3	2	1	0	0	1	2	3

6. Community-based instruction is available as one option within the special education program offerings, including the vocational, independent living, personal–social, and leisure and recreation components of the program.

Value				Current Status			
Critical	Important	Somewhat Useful	Not Important	Completely Achieved	Mostly Achieved	Partially Achieved	Not Achieved
3	2	1	0	0	1	2	3

7. Instructional procedures for students with disabilities are designed to ensure that students can perform skills they have learned in new settings (generalization) and also remember how to use their skills over time (maintenance).

Value				Current Status			
Critical	Important	Somewhat Useful	Not Important	Completely Achieved	Mostly Achieved	Partially Achieved	Not Achieved
3	2	1	0	0	1	2	3

8. Appropriate secondary curriculum materials are available for providing instruction to students with all levels of disabilities.

Value				Current Status			
Critical	Important	Somewhat Useful	Not Important	Completely Achieved	Mostly Achieved	Partially Achieved	Not Achieved
3	2	1	0	0	1	2	3

9. Procedures exist for placing students into an instructional program that is tailored to their individual needs.

Value				Current Status			
Critical	Important	Somewhat Useful	Not Important	Completely Achieved	Mostly Achieved	Partially Achieved	Not Achieved
3	2	1	0	0	1	2	3

COORDINATION AND MAINSTREAMING

10. Extracurricular school activities are available for all students with disabilities.

Value				Current Status			
Critical	Important	Somewhat Useful	Not Important	Completely Achieved	Mostly Achieved	Partially Achieved	Not Achieved
3	2	1	0	0	1	2	3

11. Specific programs exist for facilitating the social integration of all students with disabilities into regular school programs and activities.

Value				Current Status			
Critical	Important	Somewhat Useful	Not Important	Completely Achieved	Mostly Achieved	Partially Achieved	Not Achieved
3	2	1	0	0	1	2	3

12. Students with disabilities have opportunities to learn the prerequisite skills needed to participate in the regular *academic* programs.

Value				Current Status			
Critical	Important	Somewhat Useful	Not Important	Completely Achieved	Mostly Achieved	Partially Achieved	Not Achieved
3	2	1	0	0	1	2	3

13. Students with disabilities have opportunities to learn the prerequisite skills needed to participate in the regular *vocational* programs.

Value				Current Status			
Critical	Important	Somewhat Useful	Not Important	Completely Achieved	Mostly Achieved	Partially Achieved	Not Achieved
3	2	1	0	0	1	2	3

14. Teachers of regular *academic* courses are provided with assistance in adapting their instruction to meet the needs of students with disabilities.

Value				Current Status			
Critical	Important	Somewhat Useful	Not Important	Completely Achieved	Mostly Achieved	Partially Achieved	Not Achieved
3	2	1	0	0	1	2	3

15. Teachers of regular *vocational* courses are provided with assistance in adapting their instruction to meet the needs of students with disabilities.

Value				Current Status			
Critical	Important	Somewhat Useful	Not Important	Completely Achieved	Mostly Achieved	Partially Achieved	Not Achieved
3	2	1	0	0	1	2	3

16. A process exists for enhancing program planning and administrative collaboration between special education and the regular *academic* program.

Value				Current Status			
Critical	Important	Somewhat Useful	Not Important	Completely Achieved	Mostly Achieved	Partially Achieved	Not Achieved
3	2	1	0	0	1	2	3

17. A process exists for enhancing program planning and administrative collaboration between special education and the regular *vocational* program.

Value				Current Status			
Critical	Important	Somewhat Useful	Not Important	Completely Achieved	Mostly Achieved	Partially Achieved	Not Achieved
3	2	1	0	0	1	2	3

TRANSITION

18. Information exists on community services currently available for school leavers with disabilities.

Value				Current Status			
Critical	Important	Somewhat Useful	Not Important	Completely Achieved	Mostly Achieved	Partially Achieved	Not Achieved
3	2	1	0	0	1	2	3

19. Transition goals are addressed as part of the planning process for students with disabilities.

Value				Current Status			
Critical	Important	Somewhat Useful	Not Important	Completely Achieved	Mostly Achieved	Partially Achieved	Not Achieved
3	2	1	0	0	1	2	3

20. A process exists for enhancing collaboration between special education and relevant adult agencies, in order to facilitate the successful transition of students.

Value				Current Status			
Critical	Important	Somewhat Useful	Not Important	Completely Achieved	Mostly Achieved	Partially Achieved	Not Achieved
3	2	1	0	0	1	2	3

21. Procedures exist for securing parental involvement in the transition process for their child with a disability.

Value				Current Status			
Critical	Important	Somewhat Useful	Not Important	Completely Achieved	Mostly Achieved	Partially Achieved	Not Achieved
3	2	1	0	0	1	2	3

DOCUMENTATION

22. IEPs routinely contain instructional goals, including vocational, independent living, and social and interpersonal content areas that are related to the transition needs of young adults with disabilities.

Value				Current Status			
Critical	Important	Somewhat Useful	Not Important	Completely Achieved	Mostly Achieved	Partially Achieved	Not Achieved
3	2	1	0	0	1	2	3

23. Well-defined criteria exist for identifying who may receive a regular diploma, a modified diploma, a certificate of achievement, or other school district diploma option.

Value				Current Status			
Critical	Important	Somewhat Useful	Not Important	Completely Achieved	Mostly Achieved	Partially Achieved	Not Achieved
3	2	1	0	0	1	2	3

24. Procedures exist for evaluating the *immediate impact* of instruction in terms of students' learning outcomes.

Value				Current Status			
Critical	Important	Somewhat Useful	Not Important	Completely Achieved	Mostly Achieved	Partially Achieved	Not Achieved
3	2	1	0	0	1	2	3

25. Procedures exist for conducting systematic follow-along evaluations on the community adjustment of students with disabilities who leave school by graduation, by dropping out, or by aging out.

Value				Current Status			
Critical	Important	Somewhat Useful	Not Important	Completely Achieved	Mostly Achieved	Partially Achieved	Not Achieved
3	2	1	0	0	1	2	3

ADMINISTRATIVE SUPPORT

26. The school special education coordinator, school principal, and district special education administrator are all supportive of secondary special education and transition programs.

Value				Current Status			
Critical	Important	Somewhat Useful	Not Important	Completely Achieved	Mostly Achieved	Partially Achieved	Not Achieved
3	2	1	0	0	1	2	3

27. Administrators from relevant adult service agencies are committed to working with school personnel to ensure a successful transition from school to community programs.

Value				Current Status			
Critical	Important	Somewhat Useful	Not Important	Completely Achieved	Mostly Achieved	Partially Achieved	Not Achieved
3	2	1	0	0	1	2	3

28. Administrative procedures exist for using aides, volunteers, and job coaches effectively within the secondary special education programs, both in the school and in the community.

Value				Current Status			
Critical	Important	Somewhat Useful	Not Important	Completely Achieved	Mostly Achieved	Partially Achieved	Not Achieved
3	2	1	0	0	1	2	3

29. Appropriate inservice training is regularly provided to the personnel who are responsible for secondary special education and transition programs.

Value				Current Status			
Critical	Important	Somewhat Useful	Not Important	Completely Achieved	Mostly Achieved	Partially Achieved	Not Achieved
3	2	1	0	0	1	2	3

30. Schools and adult agencies use their community transition team to monitor, evaluate, and recommend improvements for secondary special education and transition programs.

Value				Current Status			
Critical	Important	Somewhat Useful	Not Important	Completely Achieved	Mostly Achieved	Partially Achieved	Not Achieved
3	2	1	0	0	1	2	3

ADULT SERVICES AND COMMUNITY RESOURCES

31. Sufficient service programs and/or community resources are available to meet the *employment* needs of young adults with disabilities.

Value				Current Status			
Critical	Important	Somewhat Useful	Not Important	Completely Achieved	Mostly Achieved	Partially Achieved	Not Achieved
3	2	1	0	0	1	2	3

32. Sufficient service programs and/or community resources are available to meet the *residential* needs of young adults with disabilities.

Value				Current Status			
Critical	Important	Somewhat Useful	Not Important	Completely Achieved	Mostly Achieved	Partially Achieved	Not Achieved
3	2	1	0	0	1	2	3

33. Sufficient service programs and/or community resources are available to meet the *income maintenance* needs of young adults with disabilities.

Value				Current Status			
Critical	Important	Somewhat Useful	Not Important	Completely Achieved	Mostly Achieved	Partially Achieved	Not Achieved
3	2	1	0	0	1	2	3

34. Sufficient service programs and/or community resources are available to meet the *leisure* needs of young adults with disabilities.

Value				Current Status			
Critical	Important	Somewhat Useful	Not Important	Completely Achieved	Mostly Achieved	Partially Achieved	Not Achieved
3	2	1	0	0	1	2	3

35. Sufficient service programs and/or community resources are available to meet the *postsecondary education* needs of young adults with disabilities.

Value				Current Status			
Critical	Important	Somewhat Useful	Not Important	Completely Achieved	Mostly Achieved	Partially Achieved	Not Achieved
3	2	1	0	0	1	2	3

36. Sufficient service programs and/or community resources are available to meet the *social support* needs of young adults with disabilities.

Value				Current Status			
Critical	Important	Somewhat Useful	Not Important	Completely Achieved	Mostly Achieved	Partially Achieved	Not Achieved
3	2	1	0	0	1	2	3

37. Sufficient service programs and/or community resources are available to meet the *health care* needs of young adults with disabilities.

Value				Current Status			
Critical	Important	Somewhat Useful	Not Important	Completely Achieved	Mostly Achieved	Partially Achieved	Not Achieved
3	2	1	0	0	1	2	3

38. Sufficient service programs and/or community resources are available to meet the *transportation* needs of young adults with disabilities.

Value				Current Status			
Critical	Important	Somewhat Useful	Not Important	Completely Achieved	Mostly Achieved	Partially Achieved	Not Achieved
3	2	1	0	0	1	2	3

RATER'S INFORMATION

Name: ______________________________ Date: ______________

Transition Team Location: ______________________________

Agency Affiliation: ______________________________

Parent of a child with a disability: Yes ☐ No ☐

Employer of a person with a disability: Yes ☐ No ☐

APPENDIX D

Sample Draft Annual Plan

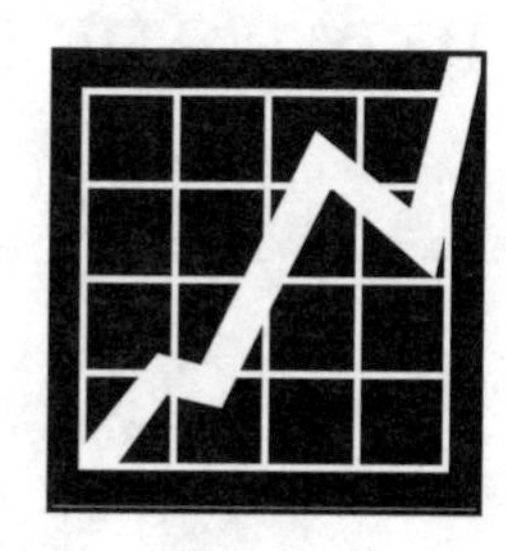

Community Transition Team

Goals and Objectives Included in the Draft Annual Plan

Fiscal Year: ____________

SUMMARY OF GOALS AND OBJECTIVES

Goal 1: Students with disabilities receive appropriate vocational instruction, which prepares them for jobs in their community.

Objective(s):

1.1: Information will be collected on the types of vocational instruction currently provided to students with disabilities.

Goal 2: Information exists on community services currently available for school leavers with disabilities.

Objective(s):

2.1: A transition manual will be developed that documents adult service programs and community resources available to individuals with disabilities.

Goal 3: Sufficient service programs and/or community resources are available to meet the transportation needs of young adults with disabilities.

Objective(s):

3.1: Current transportation programs and/or community resources for young adults with disabilities will be reviewed.

DETAILS OF THE DRAFT ANNUAL PLAN

Goal 1: Students with disabilities receive appropriate vocational instruction, which prepares them for jobs in their community.

Objective 1.1: Information will be collected on the types of vocational instruction currently provided to students with disabilities.

Subcommittee Chair: ______________________________

Street: ______________________________

City/State/Zip: ______________________________

Phone: ______________________________

Subcommittee Co-Chair: ______________________________

Street: ______________________________

City/State/Zip: ______________________________

Phone: ______________________________

Others Involved: ____

____

____

Resources Needed to Accomplish Objective

Personnel? ____________________ Office Supplies? ____________________

Duplicating? ____________________ Telephone? ____________________

Postage? ____________________ Printing? ____________________

Other? ____________________ Other? ____________________

Tasks and Timelines Needed to Accomplish Objective

Task 1: Review forms and procedures used by other transition teams to collect information on vocational instruction.

Desired Deadline: 11/01/99

Task 2: Develop a plan for collecting information on vocational instruction currently provided to students with disabilities, which includes (a) the people who will collect the information, (b) the population of students who will be surveyed, (c) the format to be used to collect the information, and (d) the timelines for collecting the information.

Desired Deadline: 12/01/99

Task 3: Meet with special education and vocational education teachers, and other key team members to discuss the plan and obtain their input and support.

Desired Deadline: 01/01/00

Task 4: Collect and summarize the information on vocational instruction.

Desired Deadline: 02/01/00

Task 5: Present the information to appropriate people (e.g., school administration), and obtain support for developing or expanding vocational instruction for students with disabilities.

Desired Deadline: 02/15/00

DETAILS OF THE DRAFT ANNUAL PLAN

Goal 2: Information exists on community services currently available for school leavers with disabilities.

Objective 2.1: A transition manual will be developed that documents adult service programs and community resources available to individuals with disabilities.

Subcommittee Chair: ______________________________

Street: ______________________________

City/State/Zip: ______________________________

Phone: ______________________________

Subcommittee Co-Chair: ______________________________

Street: ______________________________

City/State/Zip: ______________________________

Phone: ______________________________

Others Involved: ____

____

____

Resources Needed to Accomplish Objective

Personnel? ____________________ Office Supplies? ____________________

Duplicating? ____________________ Telephone? ____________________

Postage? ____________________ Printing? ____________________

Other? ____________________ Other? ____________________

Tasks and Timelines Needed to Accomplish Objective

Task 1: Gather examples of transition manuals from other transition teams, if they are available.

Desired Deadline: 01/01/00

Task 2: Review the examples to identify a format for the manual that can be adopted or adapted to meet local needs.

Desired Deadline: 01/15/00

Task 3: Develop a plan for creating the manual that includes (a) the local transition resources that should be included in the manual, (b) the types of information to be collected on each resource, and (c) the resources needed for printing and distributing the manual.

Desired Deadline: 02/01/00

Task 4: Meet with the transition team to discuss the plan for producing the manual and obtain their input.

Desired Deadline: 03/01/00

Task 5: Collect the information and produce a draft of the manual.

Desired Deadline: 04/01/00

Task 6: Review the manual with key personnel from the transition team and edit as needed.

Desired Deadline: 05/01/00

Task 7: Print the manual.

Desired Deadline: 05/15/00

Task 8: Develop a plan for disseminating the manual, and provide training to the people who will use the manual.

Desired Deadline: 05/15/00

DETAILS OF THE DRAFT ANNUAL PLAN

Goal 3: **Sufficient service programs and/or community resources are available to meet the transportation needs of young adults with disabilities.**

Objective 3.1: **Current transportation programs and/or community resources for young adults with disabilities will be reviewed.**

Subcommittee Chair: ______________________________

Street: ______________________________

City/State/Zip: ______________________________

Phone: ______________________________

Subcommittee Co-Chair: ______________________________

Street: ______________________________

City/State/Zip: ______________________________

Phone: ______________________________

Others Involved: ____

____

____

Resources Needed to Accomplish Objective

Personnel? ____________________ Office Supplies? ____________________

Duplicating? ____________________ Telephone? ____________________

Postage? ____________________ Printing? ____________________

Other? ____________________ Other? ____________________

Tasks and Timelines Needed to Accomplish Objective

Task 1: Review forms and procedures used by other transition teams to collect information on transportation resources.

Desired Deadline: 09/01/99

Task 2: Develop a plan for collecting the information that includes (a) the people who will collect the information, (b) the programs that will be surveyed, (c) the timelines for collecting the information, and (d) how the information will be presented.

Desired Deadline: 10/01/99

Task 3: Meet with transition team members and other adult service providers to review the plan and obtain their input and support.

Desired Deadline: 10/15/99

Task 4: Gather information on local transportation services that are available to young adults with disabilities.

Desired Deadline: 12/01/99

Task 5: Review the information and identify (a) the types of services that are available (e.g., public transportation, taxi, specialized vans for elderly or disabled), (b) the costs of the services, and (c) the routes that are covered.

Desired Deadline: 01/01/00

Task 6: Present the information to transition team members, and obtain their support for developing or expanding transportation resources for young adults with disabilities.

Desired Deadline: 02/01/00

APPENDIX E

Sample Task/Time Calendar

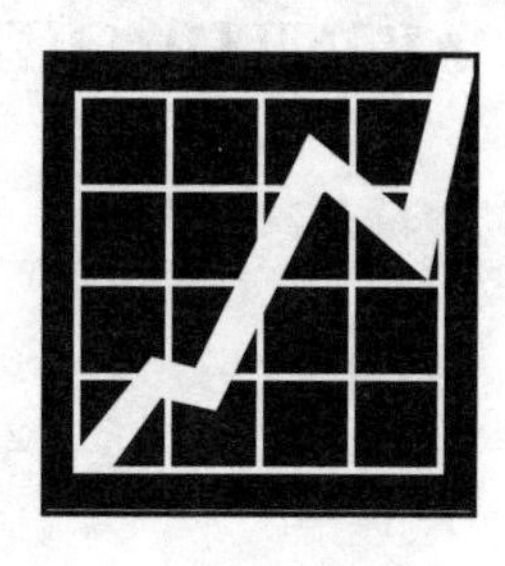

Community Transition Team

Task/Time Calendar for Draft Annual Plan

Fiscal Year:____________

MONTH: SEPTEMBER 1999

Objective		Tasks	Deadline	Complete
3.1				
	1.	Review forms and procedures used by other transition teams to collect information on transportation resources.	09/01/99	________

MONTH: OCTOBER 1999

Objective		Tasks	Deadline	Complete
3.1				
	2.	Develop a plan for collecting the information that includes (a) the people who will collect the information, (b) the programs that will be surveyed, (c) the timelines for collecting the information, and (d) how the information will be presented.	10/01/99	________
	3.	Meet with transition team members and other adult service providers to review the plan and obtain their input and support.	10/15/99	________

MONTH: NOVEMBER 1999

Objective		Tasks	Deadline	Complete
1.1				
	1.	Review forms and procedures used by other transition teams to collect information on vocational instruction.	11/01/99	________

MONTH: DECEMBER 1999

Objective		Tasks	Deadline	Complete
1.1				
	2.	Develop a plan for collecting information on vocational instruction currently provided to students with disabilities, which includes (a) the people who will collect the information, (b) the population of students who will be surveyed, (c) the format to be used to collect the information, and (d) the timelines for collecting the information.	12/01/99	________
3.1				
	4.	Gather information on local transportation services that are available to young adults with disabilities.	12/01/99	________

MONTH: JANUARY 2000

Objective		Tasks	Deadline	Complete
1.1				
	3.	Meet with special education and vocational education teachers, and other key team members to discuss the plan and obtain their input and support.	01/01/00	________
2.1				
	1.	Gather examples of transition manuals from other transition teams, if they are available.	01/01/00	________
	2.	Review the examples to identify a format for the manual that can be adopted or adapted to meet local needs.	01/15/00	________
3.1				
	5.	Review the information and identify (a) the types of services that are available (e.g., public transportation, taxi, specialized vans for elderly or disabled), (b) the costs of the services, and (c) the routes that are covered.	01/01/00	________

MONTH: FEBRUARY 2000

Objective		Tasks	Deadline	Complete
1.1				
	4.	Collect and summarize the information on vocational instruction.	02/01/00	________
	5.	Present the information to appropriate people (e.g., school administration), and obtain support for developing or expanding vocational instruction for students with disabilities.	02/15/00	________
2.1				
	3.	Develop a plan for creating the manual that includes (a) the local transition resources that should be included in the manual, (b) the types of information to be collected on each resource, and (c) the resources needed for printing and distributing the manual.	02/01/00	________
3.1				
	6.	Present the information to transition team members, and obtain their support for developing or expanding transportation resources for young adults with disabilities.	02/01/00	________

MONTH: MARCH 2000

Objective		Tasks	Deadline	Complete
2.1				
	4.	Meet with the transition team to discuss the plan for producing the manual and obtain their input.	03/01/00	________

MONTH: APRIL 2000

Objective		Tasks	Deadline	Complete
2.1				
	5.	Collect the information and produce a draft of the manual.	04/01/00	________

MONTH: MAY 2000

Objective		Tasks	Deadline	Complete
2.1				
	6.	Review the manual with key personnel from the transition team and edit as needed.	05/01/00	________
	7.	Print the manual.	05/15/00	________
	8.	Develop a plan for disseminating the manual, and provide training to the people who will use the manual.	05/15/00	________

References

Americans with Disabilities Act of 1990, 42 U.S.C. § 12101 *et seq.*

Benz, M. R., Lindstrom, L., & Halpern, A. S. (1995). Mobilizing local communities to improve transition services. *Career Development for Exceptional Individuals, 18,* 21–32.

Benz, M. R., Lindstrom, L. E., Halpern, A. S., & Rothstrom, R. S. (1991). *Community transition team model: Facilitator's manual.* Eugene: University of Oregon Press.

Blalock, G. (1990). *New Mexico School-to-Work Transition Project: Demonstration project in transition of youth with disabilities from school to work and postsecondary training.* Unpublished manuscript, University of New Mexico, Albuquerque.

Blalock, G. (1996). Community transition teams as the foundation for transition services for youth with disabilities. *Journal of Learning Disabilities, 29*(2), 148–159.

Carl, J. (no date). *The team building workbook.* In support of the Iowa Transition Initiative Transition Process Model. Grinnell, IA: Organizational Development Consultant.

Cozzens, G., Dowdy, C. A., & Smith, T. E. C. (1999). *Adult agencies: Linkages for adolescents in transition.* Austin, TX: PRO-ED.

Cronin, M. E., & Patton, J. R. (1993). *Life skills instruction for all students with special needs: A practical guide for integrating real-life content into the curriculum.* Austin, TX: PRO-ED.

Delbecq, A. L., Van de Ven, A. H., & Gustafson, D. H. (1975). *Group techniques for program planning: A guide to nominal group and delphi processes.* Glenview, IL: Scott, Foresman.

Halpern, A. S., Benz, M. R., & Lindstrom, L. E. (1992). A systems change approach to improving secondary special education and transition programs at the community level. *Career Development for Exceptional Individuals, 15,* 109–120.

Halpern, A. S., Lindstrom, L. E., Benz, M. R., & Rothstrom, R. S. (1991). *Community transition team model: Needs assessment instrument.* Eugene: University of Oregon Press.

Helge, D. (1991). *Rural, exceptional, at risk.* Reston, VA: Council for Exceptional Children.

Individuals with Disabilities Education Act Amendments of 1991, 20 U.S.C. § 1400 *et seq.*

Mahler, M., & Brustein, M. (1997). *New Mexico school-to-work implementation manual.* Santa Fe, NM: Governor's Office.

National Transition Network. (1996–1997, Winter). Transition systems change and school-to-work: Emerging areas of collaboration. *Network News,* pp. 1, 3, 6.

Navarrete, L. A., & White, W. J. (1994). School to community transition planning: Factors to consider when working with culturally diverse students and families in rural settings. *Rural Special Education Quarterly, 13*(1), 51–56.

New Mexico State Department of Education. (1996). *Educational Plan for Student Success.* Santa Fe: Author.

Region IX Education Cooperative. (1997). *Memorandum of Understanding among the Developmental Disabilities Division, Mental Health Division, Division of Vocational Rehabilitation, Department of Labor, Social Security Administration, Area Community Colleges, and Schools Districts in the Region IX Education Cooperative.* Ruidoso, NM: Author.

Rehabilitation Act of 1973, 29 U.S.C. § 701 *et seq.*

Smith, G., & Edelen-Smith, P. (1993). Restructuring secondary special education Hawaiian style. *Intervention in School and Clinic, 28,* 247, 248–252.

Transition Assistance Project. (1996a, Summer). CTICs address multilingual materials, meeting style. *What's Working in Transition?* p. 3. (Available from University of Minnesota, College of Education and Human Development).

Transition Assistance Project. (1996b, Spring). Holding meetings that are worth attending. *What's Working in Transition?* p. 6. (Available from University of Minnesota, College of Education and Human Development).

Transition Assistance Project. (1997a, Winter). The art of networking. *What's Working in Transition?* p. 6. (Available from University of Minnesota, College of Education and Human Development).

Transition Assistance Project. (1997b, Winter). The CTIC top ten list. *What's Working in Transition?* p. 3. (Available from University of Minnesota, College of Education and Human Development).

Transition Assistance Project. (1998a, Summer). CTIC activity updates. *What's Working in Transition?* p. 3. (Available from University of Minnesota, College of Education and Human Development).

Transition Assistance Project. (1998b, Summer). Learning and earning: Partnerships with employers. *What's Working in Transition?* pp. 4–5. (Available from University of Minnesota, College of Education and Human Development).

Notes

Notes